DISCOVERING

BRUGES
BRUGGE BRUGES BRÜGGE

PHOTOGRAPHS FOTO'S PHOTOS AUFNAHMEN
VINCENT MERCKX

TEXT TEKSTEN TEXTES TEXTE
GEORGES-HENRI DUMONT

HET Middeleeuwse Brugge bouwt verder op het Romeinse Brugge waarvan het *castrum* waarschijnlijk de vierkante vorm verleende aan de Burg. Maar de stichter van de stad, die toen *Bryggia* of *Bruccia* heette, was zonder enige twijfel Boudewijn met de IJzeren Arm, de eerste Graaf van Vlaanderen (862-879). Hij bouwde een burcht die werd verdedigd enerzijds door de rivier Reie, anderzijds door een stenen muur met torens en poorten. Deze versterkte vesting deed dienst bij het militair verzet tegen de Noormannen. In de 11de eeuw bouwde Robrecht de Fries (1071-1093) een nieuw kasteel op de plaats van het huidige Justitiepaleis. Het omvatte een kapel, eerst ter ere van de maagd, daarna van de Heilige Donaas toen zijn relieken daarheen werden gebracht.

Terwijl het administratieve leven zich ontwikkelde rond de grafelijke residentie, nam de bevolkingsaangroei toe in de stad, die zich in concentrische cirkels uitbreidde. De parochie van de Sint-Salvatorkerk bevond zich trouwens buiten de eerste omwalling, die *grosso modo* overeenkomt met de binnenkanalen. De commerciële activiteiten namen een steeds grotere uitbreiding. Brugse handelaars gingen zelf naar het buitenland om er te kopen en te verkopen. Vanaf het begin van de 12de eeuw kwamen Denen en Italianen naar Brugge om er het Vlaamse laken te laden, ze brachten het tot in Novgorod en in het Middelandse Zeegebied. Deze trend zette zich verder door: de schepen van de Hanze en uit alle hoeken van het Westen legden in Brugge aan en Brugge werd een Europese commerciële metropool.

De rijkdom en de trots van de bourgeoisie verplichtte de prinsen ertoe met hen te onderhandelen over de uitbreiding van de autonomie van de stad. Met het charter van 1127 schafte de graaf de grondbelasting af en kende hij de schepenen administratieve functies toe, evenals de mogelijkheid om hun gewoonterecht aan te passen. Door haar geprivilegieerde statuut, haar eigen instellingen en het besef van collectiviteit, vormde Brugge van dan af een gemeenschap. Het belfort, dat sinds 1282 boven de hallen uittorent, is het symbool van haar macht.

De graaf Gwijde van Dampierre (1278-1305) was, zoals zijn voorgangers, vasal van de koning van Frankrijk. Hij verzette zich tegen Filips IV de Schone, die probeerde zijn autoriteit te verzwakken en zich daarom opwierp als beschermheer van de patriciërs van de grote steden in Vlaanderen. Tot het uiterste gedreven door die constante bemoeienissen, onthief de graaf van Vlaanderen zich van zijn feodale verplichtingen en allieerde hij zich met Engeland. De koning van Frankrijk reageerde met een inval in het graafschap en de annexering aan het koninklijke domein; Gwijde van Dampierre werd gedwongen tot capitulatie en gevangen gezet in Compiègne. Filips De Schone kwam Brugge binnen op 28 mei 1301. Bij zijn vertrek liet hij de stad onder de heerschappij van een bijzonder onhandige goeverneur, Jacques de Châtillon, die zich al snel allieerde met de rijke patriciërs – de *Leliaarts*, een allusie op de Franse lelie – en meteen nieuwe belastingen hief. De ontevredenheid van het volk werd alras algemeen. De "ambachten" waren reeds lang gebrand op het breken van de exclusieve macht van de patriciërs en zagen hun kans. Een eerste opstand brak los en werd bloedig neergeslagen door de Fransen. Dat was de druppel die de emmer deed overlopen. In de vroege ochtend van de 18e mei 1302 begonnen de *Klauwaarts* – een allusie op de klauwen van de leeuw van Vlaanderen – met het doden van de schildwachten, zij namen bezit van de poorten en vermoordden de Franse bezetters. Ondertussen had de familie van graaf Gwijde van Dampierre, die nog steeds in gevangenschap verbleef, het Vlaamse verzet georganiseerd. Guillaume de Juliers en de graaf van Namen schaarden zich aan de zijde van de Brugse volkstribuun Pieter De Coninc en brachten een leger op de been, dat weldra versterkt werd met een handvol trouwe leenheren. De beweging was oorspronkelijk zuiver sociaal, maar kreeg een nationaal karakter. Onder de vlag van de graaf vernietigden de Vlamingen het leger van de koning van Frankrijk op 11 juli 1302 bij de muren van Kortrijk. Zevenhonderd gulden sporen van Franse ruiters werden op het slagveld opgeraapt, waardoor de slag zijn naam kreeg.

Vlaanderen was bevrijd, de sociale oorsprong van het conflict won weer aan belang. Het werd de ondergang van de patriciërs en de *Leliaarts* ten voordele van de ambachten en de *Klauwaarts*. De graaf, die aan hen zijn herintrede te danken had, verklaarde het patriciërsmonopolie ten einde en kende in 1304 een nieuw vrijhandelscharter toe als bewijs van de triomf van de democratie.

Ondanks de problemen die werden veroorzaakt door de verzanding van de toegang naar de zee maar dankzij de voorhaven van Damme, bereikte Brugge in de 14de en 15de eeuw het hoogtepunt van haar welvaart en uitstraling. Zeventien naties hadden er hun kantoren, waaronder Venetiërs, Genuezen en Firenzers, Engelsen en Schotten, Portugezen, Castilianen en Basken. Onder de hertogen van Bourgondië kende Brugge een periode van stabiliteit. Het architecturale decor straalde in al zijn luister met het stadhuis, de voltooiing van de Onze-Lieve-Vrouwkerk en de Sint-Salvatorkerk, evenals van het Sint-Janshospitaal, de uitbreiding van de Sint-Jacobskerk, de verhoging van het belfort, de bouw van het Gruuthusepaleis, vele patricierswoningen en gildenhuizen. De welvaart van de stad had de grootste schilders ertoe aangezet hier hun ateliers op te trekken. Hiertoe behoorden Jan van Eyck, Petrus Christus, Hans Memling, Gerard David, Hugo van der Goes.

In de 16de eeuw stond Brugge haar rol van commerciële metropool af aan Antwerpen. Maar de stad bleef haar artistieke uitstraling behouden. Op 10 april 1515 deed Keizer Karel zijn Blijde Intrede onder de Renaissance triomfbogen, een stijl die in Brugge nadrukkelijker aanwezig was dan in andere steden van de voormalige Nederlanden. Bewijzen daarvan zijn de schouw van het Landhuis van het Vrije in Brugge, de portiek van de Heilige Bloedbasiliek en de voorgevel van de Oude Griffie.

Tijdens de politiek-religieuze revolutie tegen de Spaanse koning Filips II raakte de fanatieke beeldenstorm van de calvinisten Brugge net zo hard als de rest van het land. De voorspoedige periode tijdens de heerschappij van de aartshertogen Albrecht en Isabella gaf de gelegenheid om de geplunderde kerken te restaureren en nieuwe kerken in barokstijl te bouwen. Maar de Spaanse mislukking en de bezetting van Brugge door de troepen van Lodewijk XIV vertraagden de heropbouw tot de aanstelling van het Oostenrijkse regime in 1715. Onder de heerschappij van keizerin Maria-Theresia (1740-1780) en de regering van haar schoonbroer Karel van Lotharingen hernam de economische bloei met het graven van een haven voor zeeschepen, de oprichting van nieuwe industrieën, de mode van het kantwerk dat voornamelijk door begijntjes werd gemaakt.

De verovering door de Franse republikeinen, die de Romaanse Sint-Donaaskerk vernielden, bracht een zekere lethargie over Brugge, dat hoofdstad van het departement Lys was geworden.

De industriële revolutie van de 19de eeuw beïnvloedde de stad nauwelijks, waardoor ze gespaard bleef van de kwalijke gevolgen van een wilde urbanisatie. Gelukkig ijverde koning Leopold II actief voor de aanleg van de haven van Zeebrugge, die een nieuwe aanknoping met de welvaart zou vormen. Helaas, nauwelijks waren de werken beëindigd toen het Duitse leger een deel van de kust in bezit nam: van 1914 tot 1918 deed Zeebrugge dienst als oorlogshaven. En tweeëntwintig jaar later werden de haveninstallaties opnieuw bezet door vijandelijke torpedojagers, onderzeeërs en wachtschepen. Maar de opleving na de Tweede Wereldoorlog was, meer nog dan die na de Eerste, beslissend. Dankzij haar haven op de Noordzee heroverde Brugge haar plaats in de internationale handel.

Tegelijkertijd begonnen de machthebbers in de stad aan een politiek van restauratie en heropleving van het architecturale patrimonium van Brugge. Ze moesten er niettemin gebouwen in hedendaagse stijl aan toevoegen. Dit samengaan van het heden met het verleden is niet altijd vanzelfsprekend, maar noodzakelijk om tegelijk te voldoen aan de behoeften van het moderne leven en de verwachtingen van de duizenden bezoekers die naar Brugge komen omdat daar de meest prestigieuze verzameling van cultuurschoonheid te vinden is.

L A Bruges médiévale continue une Bruges romaine dont le *castrum* donna probablement à la place du Burg sa forme carrée. Mais le fondateur de la ville, qui s'appelait alors *Bryggia* ou *Bruccia*, fut incontestablement Baudouin Bras-de-Fer, premier comte de Flandre (862-879). Il construisit une forteresse défendue à la fois par la rivière Reie et par une muraille en pierre avec tours et portes. Cette place forte servit à la résistance militaire contre les Normands. Au XIe siècle, Robert le Frison (1071-1093) édifia un nouveau château, à l'endroit du palais du Franc de Bruges place du Burg. Il comportait une chapelle d'abord consacrée à la vierge, puis à saint Donatien quand ses reliques y furent transférées.

Tandis que la vie administrative se développait autour de la résidence comtale, la population ne cessait de croître dans la ville qui s'étendait en cercles concentriques. La paroisse de l'église Saint-Sauveur se situait d'ailleurs au-delà de la première enceinte, qui correspond *grosso modo* aux canaux intérieurs (Dyver, Groenerei, speigelrei…). Les activités commerciales prenaient de plus en plus d'ampleur. Les marchands brugeois se rendaient eux-mêmes à l'étranger pour y vendre et acheter. Dès le début du XIIe siècle, Danois et Italiens venaient à Bruges pour y charger les draps de Flandre; ils les acheminaient jusqu'à Novgorod et dans le monde méditerranéen. Cette tendance ne cessa de s'accentuer : les navires de la Hanse et de tous les coins de l'Occident affluèrent au port et Bruges devint une métropole commerciale européenne.

La richesse et la fierté des bourgeois obligèrent les princes à négocier avec eux l'élargissement de l'autonomie urbaine. Par la charte de 1127, le comte abandonna la perception de l'impôt foncier et attribua aux échevins des fonctions administratives, ainsi que la faculté de modifier leur droit coutumier. Par son statut privilégié, ses institutions propres et la conscience de former une collectivité, Bruges constitua désormais une commune. Le beffroi qui depuis 1282 se dresse au-dessus des halles symbolisait sa puissance.

Le comte Gui de Dampierre (1278-1305) était, comme ses prédécesseurs, le vassal du roi de France. Il s'opposa à Philippe IV le Bel qui s'ingéniait à diminuer son autorité et, à cet effet, se posait en protecteur des patriciens des grandes villes de Flandre. Poussé à bout par ces ingérences continues, le comte de Flandre se déclara délié de ses devoirs féodaux et s'allia à l'Angleterre. Le roi de France réagit en envahissant le comté et en l'annexant au domaine royal. Contraint à capituler, Gui de Dampierre fut emprisonné à Compiègne. Philippe le Bel entra à Bruges le 28 mai 1301. À son départ, il laissa la ville sous le pouvoir d'un gouverneur particulièrement maladroit, Jacques de Châtillon, qui s'empressa de s'allier avec les riches patriciens – les *Leliaarts*, par allusion au lys de France – et s'empressa de lever de nouveaux impôts. Le mécontentement populaire se généralisa promptement. Les «métiers», depuis longtemps impatients de renverser le pouvoir exclusif des patriciens, relevèrent la tête. Une première émeute éclata; elle fut cruellement réprimée par les Français. C'en était trop. À l'aube du 18 mai 1302, les *Klauwaarts* – allusion aux griffes (*klauwen*) du lion de Flandre – tuèrent les sentinelles, s'emparèrent des portes et massacrèrent les occupants français. Entre-temps, la famille du comte Gui de Dampierre toujours captif n'avait pas tardé à organiser la résistance flamande. Guillaume de Juliers et le comte de Namur se joignirent au tribun brugeois Pierre de Coninc et mirent sur pied une armée, bientôt renforcée par une poignée de seigneurs restés fidèles. Purement social au départ, le mouvement prit dès lors un caractère national et c'est sous la bannière du comte que les Flamands écrasèrent l'armée du roi de France le 11 juillet 1302 sous les murs de Courtrai. Sept cents éperons d'or de cavaliers français furent ramassés sur le champs de bataille et donnèrent à celle-ci son nom.

La Flandre étant libérée, l'origine sociale du conflit reprit force. Ce fut la déconfiture des patriciens et des *Leliaarts* au profit des métiers et des *Klauwaarts*. Le comte, qui devait à ceux-ci sa restauration, fit proclamer la fin du monopole des patriciens et accorda, en 1304, une nouvelle charte de franchise consacrant le triomphe de la démocratie.

En dépit des problèmes résultant de l'ensablement de l'accès à la mer et grâce à l'avant-port de Damme, Bruges atteignit aux XIVe et XVe siècles l'apogée de sa prospérité et de son rayonnement. Dix-sept nations y avaient leur comptoir parmi lesquels les Vénitiens, les Génois et les Florentins, les Anglais et les Écossais, les Portugais, les Castillans et les Basques. Sous les ducs de Bourgogne, Bruges connut une période de stabilité. Son décor architectural avait pris toute sa magnificence avec l'hôtel de ville, l'achèvement des églises Notre-Dame et Saint-Sauveur, celui de l'hôpital Saint-Jean, l'agrandissement de l'église Saint-Jacques, la surélévation du beffroi, la construction du palais Gruuthuse, de nombreux hôtels patriciens et maisons corporatives. La prospérité de la ville avait incité les plus grands peintres à y installer leurs ateliers. C'était le cas de Jan van Eyck, Petrus Christus, Hans Memling, Gérard David, Hugo van der Goes.

Au XVIe siècle, Bruges abandonna son rôle de métropole commerciale désormais détenu par Anvers. Mais elle ne perdit pas pour autant son rayonnement artistique. Le 10 avril 1515, l'empereur Charles Quint fit sa Joyeuse Entrée sous les arcs de triomphe Renaissance, un style qui, davantage que dans les autres villes des anciens Pays-Bas, s'imposa à Bruges comme en témoignent notamment la cheminée du palais du Franc de Bruges, le portail de la basilique du Saint-Sang et la façade du Greffe civil.

Au temps de la révolution politico-religieuse contre le roi d'Espagne Philippe II, le fanatisme iconoclaste des calvinistes toucha Bruges comme le reste du pays. La parenthèse heureuse du règne des archiducs Albert et Isabelle fut l'occasion de restaurer les églises saccagées et d'en construire de nouvelle, dans le style baroque.

La débâcle espagnole et l'occupation de Bruges par les troupes de Louis XIV retardèrent le redressement jusqu'à l'instauration du régime autrichien en 1715. Sous le règne de l'impératrice Marie-Thérèse (1740-1780) et le gouvernement général de son beau-frère Charles de Lorraine, une reprise économique s'esquissa par le creusement d'un bassin pour navires de haute mer, la création de nouvelles industries, la vogue de la dentelles produite principalement par les béguines.

La conquête par les républicains français, outre la destruction de l'église romane Saint-Donatien, entraîna la léthargie de Bruges, devenue chef-lieu du département de la Lys.

La révolution industrielle du XIXe siècle n'atteignit guère la ville, ce qui lui épargna les méfaits d'un urbanisme sauvage. Heureusement le roi Léopold II œuvra activement en faveur de l'aménagement du port de Zeebrugge, qui devait permettre de renouer avec la prospérité.

Hélas ! les travaux à peine achevés, l'armée allemande s'empara d'une partie de la côte : de 1914 à 1918, Zeebrugge servit de port de guerre. Et, vingt-deux ans plus tard, torpilleurs, sous-marins et vedettes ennemies occupèrent à nouveau les installations portuaires. Mais, davantage que le réveil après la Première Guerre mondiale, celui qui suivit la Seconde s'avéra décisif. Grâce au port sur la mer du Nord, Bruges reconquit sa place dans le commerce international.

Pendant ce temps-là, les pouvoirs urbains commençaient à mener une politique de restauration et de revitalisation du patrimoine architectural de Bruges. Il leur fallut cependant y insérer des bâtiments de style contemporain. Cette coexistence du présent et du passé n'est pas toujours évidente. Elle s'impose toutefois pour satisfaire à la fois les besoins de la vie moderne et l'attente des milliers de visiteurs qui viennent à Bruges, et s'y attardent parce-qu'elle est le plus prestigieux reposoir de la beauté.

Het Walplein
La Walplein
The Walplein
Der Walplein

MEDIÆVAL Bruges grew up of Roman Bruges whose *castrum* most likely gave the Burgplein its square shape. *Bryggia* or *Bruccia*, as the founder of the city was known, was undoubtedly Baudouin Iron-Arm, the first Count of Flanders (862-879). He built a fortress defended by both the river Reie and by a stone wall with towers and gates. This fortified enclosure was erected against the Vikings. In the 11th century Robert the Frisian built a new castle on the site of the Palace of the County of Bruges (the *Brugse Vrije*) on the Burg square. Its chapel was originally dedicated to the Virgin and then later to Saint Donatien when his relics were transferred there.

While administrative activity developed around the Count's residence the population continued to increase and the city expanded in concentric circles. Thus the parish of the church of the Holy Redeemer was outside the first walls which more or less corresponded to the inner canals of the Dyver, Groenerei, Spiegelrei etc. Commerce became more and more developed, the merchants of Bruges themselves travelling abroad to buy and sell. From the early 12th century Danes and Italians came to Bruges for Flanders cloth which they distributed as far as Novgorod and the Mediterranean basin. This commerce became even more important as the ships of the Hanseatic League and from all corners of the West came to the port, making Bruges a European commercial metropolis.

The wealth and pride of the burghers obliged the princes to negotiate with them on questions of urban autonomy and power sharing. By the charter of 1127 the Count relinquished control of property taxes and gave the magistrates responsibility for public administration and the right to modify their customary laws. With its privileged status, its own institutions and its collective interests, Bruges thus became a municipality. The belfry erected over the Cloth hall in 1282 symbolized the power of the city.

Like his predecessors Count Guy de Dampierre (1278-1305) was a vassal of the King of France. He opposed King Philip IV le Bel who tried to undermine his authority by posing as the protector of the large towns of Flanders. Pushed to the limit by Philip's continual meddling the Count declared himself quit of his feudal obligations and allied himself with England. The King retaliated by invading the County and annexing it to the royal domain. Forced to sur-

render, Guy de Dampierre was imprisoned in Compiègne. Philip entered Bruges on May 28, 1301. He left the city in the hands of a particularity inept governor, Jacques de Châtillon, who allied himself with the rich patricians – the *Leliaarts*, an allusion to the lilies of France – and quickly raised new taxes. Popular unrest quickly grew. The guilds who had long wished to diminish the exclusive power of the patricians banded together. A first protest was raised and brutally repressed by the French. That was the turning point. At dawn on May 18, 1302 the *Klauwaarts* – an allusion to the claws of the Flemish lion – killed the sentries, seized the gates and massacred the French occupants. In the meantime the family of Count Guy de Dampierre who was still in prison had busily organized the Flemish resistance. Guillaume de Juliers and the Count of Namur joined with the popular orator Pierre de Coninc and raised an army, soon reinforced by a handful of faithful lords. Although purely social at first the movement took on a national character and it was under the Count's banner that the Flemish crushed the French army outside Kortrijk on July 11, 1302. Seven hundred golden spurs of the French knights were piled up on the battlefield, whence its name: the Battle of the Golden Spurs.

Now that Flanders was liberated the social origins of the conflict again came to the fore. The patricians and the *Leliaarts* lost power to the guilds and the *Klauwaarts*. The Count who owed his restoration to the latter proclaimed the end of the patrician monopoly and granted a new charter extending the franchise in 1304, consecrating the triumph of democracy.

Despite the problems arising from the silting up of the sea access but thanks to the outport of Damme in the 14th and 15th centuries Bruges reached the apogee of its prosperity and influence. Seventeen nations had trading posts there among whom were Venetians, Genoans, Florentines, English and Scots, Portugese, Castillians and Basques. Under the Dukes of Burgundy Bruges enjoyed a period of stability. Its architecture became very imposing with the erection of the City hall, the completion of the churches of Our Lady and the Holy Redeemer, Saint John's hospital, the enlargement of Saint James' church, the extension of the belfry, the construction of the Gruuthuse palace and numerous patrician mansions and guild halls.

The wealth of the city attracted many great artists who set up their studios there, among them Jan van Eyck, Petrus Christus, Hans Memling, Gerard David and Hugo van der Goes.

In the 16th century Bruges relinquished its role as a commercial metropolis to Antwerp, but still retained its artistic influence. On April 10, 1515 Emperor Charles V made his *Joyeuse Entrée* beneath Renaissance triumphal arches, a style that was adopted more quickly in Bruges than in the other cities of the former Low Countries as may be seen in the mantelpiece of the palace of the Franc of Bruges, the portal of the Holy Blood basilica of the Civil Registry.

As the time of the politico-religious revolt against King Philip II of Spain the fury of the iconoclasts fell upon Bruges as well as the rest of the country. The peaceful period of Archdukes Albert and Isabella made it possible to restore the churches that were sacked and defaced and to build new ones in the baroque style.

The disastrous Spanish reign and the occupation of Bruges by the troops of Louis XIV of France delayed recovery until the Austrian regime commenced in 1715. Under the reign of Empress Maria Theresa (1740-1780) and the government of her brother-in-law Charles of Lorraine a slight economic recovery began, launched by the digging of a basin for high seas ships, the creation of new industries and the fashion for lace produced mainly by the béguines.

The conquest by the French Republican army which led to the destruction of the Romanesque church of Saint Donatien contributed to the lethargy of Bruges, now the seat of the Department of the Lys.

The 19th century Industrial Revolution barely touched the city, thus sparing it heedless destruction and development.

Fortunately, King Leopold II worked energetically to enlarge the port of Zeebrugge which led to economic recovery. Alas, the work was barely completed when the German army seized part of the coast. From 1914 to 1918 Zeebrugge was a war port. Twenty-two years later torpedo boats, submarines and enemy cutters once again occupied the port installations. After the second World War the recovery was more successful than after World War I. Thanks to the North Sea port Bruges regained its place in international commerce.

At this time the urban authorities initiated a policy of restoration and renewal of the architectural heritage of Bruges into which new buildings in a more contemporary style had to be integrated. This coexistence of the past and the present is not always obvious but is necessary to satisfy the demands of modern life and the expectations of the thousands of people who come to Bruges and dally there, enchanted by such perfect beauty.

DAS mittelalterliche Brügge entstand über einem römischen Brügge, dessen *castrum* wahrscheinlich dem Burgplatz seine quadratische Form gab. Der Gründer der Stadt aber, die damals den Namen *Bryggia* oder *Bruccia* trug, war unbestritten Balduin "Eisenarm", der erste Graf von Flandern (862-879). Er errichtete eine durch den Fluss Reie sowie eine Steinmauer mit Türmen und Toren geschützte Festung. Diese Anlage diente dem militärischen Widerstand gegen die Normannen. Im 11. Jh. erbaute Robert der Friese (1071-1093) eine neue Burg an der Stelle des heutigen Justizpalastes. Sie umfasste eine zunächst der Jungfrau Maria und später dann nach Überführung der Reliquien dem heiligen Donatus geweihte Kapelle.

Während sich das Verwaltungsleben rund um die gräfliche Residenz entfaltete, nahm die Bevölkerung in der sich in konzentrischen Kreisen erstreckenden Stadt ständig zu. Die Gemeinde der Salvatorkirche befand sich übrigens außerhalb der ersten Umfassungsmauer, deren Verlauf in etwa dem inneren Kanälen entsprach. Die kommerziellen Aktivitäten nahmen immer größere Ausmaße an. Die Brügger Kaufleute reisten selbst ins Ausland, um dort ihre Waren abzusetzen und andere zu erstehen. Seit Anfang des 12. Jhs. kamen Dänen und Italiener nach Brügge, um Tuch von Flandern zu laden, das sie dann bis nach Novgorod und in die Mittelmeerländer transportierten. Dieses Geschäft weitete sich ständig aus: Schiffe der Hanse und aus allen Ecken der westlichen Welt liefen im Hafen ein und Brügge wurde zu einem europäischen Handelszentrum.

Der Reichtum und der Stolz der Bürger zwangen die Prinzen zu Verhandlungen über eine Ausweitung der städtischen Autonomie. Mit dem Freibrief von 1127 verzichtete der Graf auf die Erhebung der Grundsteuer, übertrug den Schöffen administrative Aufgaben und gestand ihnen die Möglichkeit zu, ihr Gewohnheitsrecht zu ändern. Dank ihres privilegierten Status, eigener Institutionen und eines Gruppenzugehörigkeitsgefühls bildete Brügge von nun an eine Kommune. Der Bergfried, der sich seit 1282 über die Tuchhallen erhebt, symbolisiert deren Stärke.

Graf Gui de Dampierre (1278-1305) war, wie seine Vorgänger auch, ein Vasall des Königs von Frankreich. Er stellte sich gegen Philipp IV.

den Schönen, der seine Autorität zu schmälern suchte und zu diesem Zwecke als Beschützer der Adligen der großen Städte Flanderns auftrat. Der durch diese ständigen Einmischungen zum Äußersten getriebene Graf von Flandern erklärte, sich nicht länger an seine Feudalpflichten gebunden zu fühlen und schloss eine Allianz mit England. Der König von Frankreich antwortete mit dem Einmarsch in die Grafschaft und der Annexion des königlichen Besitzes; zur Kapitulation gezwungen, wurde Gui de Dampierre in Compiègne gefangen gesetzt. Philipp der Schöne zog am 28. Mai 1301 in Brügge ein. Bei seinem Weggang ließ er die Stadt unter der Herrschaft eines besonders ungeschickten Gouverneurs, Jacques de Châtillon, zurück, der sich eifrig mühte, die reichen Adligen – die *Leliaarts* in Anspielung an die Lilie von Frankreich – für sich zu gewinnen und eilig neue Steuern erhob. Die Unzufriedenheit in der Bevölkerung weitete sich rasch aus. Die seit langem ungeduldig auf eine Gelegenheit zum Sturz der Alleinmacht der Adligen wartenden Gilden begannen sich zu regen. Ein erster Aufstand brach los; er wurde von den Franzosen grausam niedergeschlagen. Das brachte das Fass zum überlaufen: Im Morgengrauen des 18. Mai 1302 töteten die *Klauwaarts* – Anspielung auf die Klauen des Löwen von Flandern – die Wachposten, nahmen die Tore ein und massakrierten die französischen Besatzer. Unterdessen hatte die Familie des noch immer gefangen gehaltenen Grafen Gui de Dampierre keine Zeit verloren und den flämischen Widerstand organisiert. Guillaume de Juliers und der Graf von Namur schlossen sich dem Brügger Tribun Pierre de Coninc an und stellten eine Armee auf, die bald von einer Handvoll treu gebliebener Lehnsherren verstärkt wurde. Die anfänglich rein soziale Bewegung nahm nun einen nationalen Charakter an und am 11. Juli 1302 schlugen die Flamen unter dem Banner des Grafen die Armee des Königs von Frankreich vor den Mauern von Kortrijk vernichtend. Siebenhundert Goldsporne von französischen Reitern wurden anschließend auf dem Schlachtfeld aufgesammelt und gaben diesem seinen Namen.

Da Flandern nun befreit war, gewann der soziale Ursprung des Konflikts an Stärke. Es folgte die Niederlage der Adligen und der

Leliaarts zu Gunsten der Handwerker und der *Klauwaarts*. Der Graf, der Letzteren seine neuerliche Macht verdankte, ließ das Ende des Monopols der Adligen verkünden und bewilligte 1304 einen neuen Freibrief, der den Triumph der Demokratie krönte.

Trotz der Probleme aufgrund der Versandung des Zugangs zum Meer und dank des Vorhafens von Damme erreichte Brügge im 14. und 15. Jh. den Höhepunkt seines Wohlstands und seiner Bedeutung. Siebzehn Nationen hatten in der Stadt ihre Faktoreien, unter ihnen die Venezianer, die Genuesen und Florentiner, die Engländer und Schotten, die Portugiesen, die Kastilier und die Basken. Unter den Herzögen von Burgund erlebte Brügge eine Zeit der Stabilität. Seine Architektur hatte mit dem Rathaus, der Vollendung der Liebfrauenkirche und der Salvatorkirche, der Kirche des St. Johannes-Hospitals, der Erweiterung der Kirche St. Jakobus, der Aufstockung des Bergfrieds, dem Bau des Gruuthuse Palais sowie zahlreicher Herrensitze und Zunfthäuser die volle Pracht erreicht. Der Wohlstand der Stadt veranlasste die bedeutendsten Maler, dort ihre Ateliers einzurichten, so z.B. Jan van Eyck, Petrus Christus, Hans Memling, Gérard David und Hugo van der Goes.

Im 16. Jh. musste Brügge seine Rolle als führende Handelsmetropole an Antwerpen abtreten. Es verlor jedoch nicht seine Ausstrahlung im Bereich der Kunst. Am 10. April 1515 hielt Kaiser Karl der Fünfte seine "Joyeuse Entrée" ("Fröhlicher Einzug") unter den Triumphbögen im Renaissance-Stil ab, welcher sich als Kunstrichtung in Brügge mehr als in den anderen Städten der Alten Niederlande durchsetzte, wovon besonders der Kamin des Sitzes der Freigrafschaft von Brügge, das Portal der Heiligblut-Basilika und die Fassade der Zivilgerichtsschreiberei zeugen.

Zur Zeit der politisch-religiösen Revolution gegen den König von Spanien Philip II. erfasste der ikonoklastische Fanatismus der Calvinisten die Stadt Brügge wie auch das übrige Land. Die wohlbringende Atempause während der Herrschaft der Erzherzöge Albert und Isabel bot Gelegenheit, die verwüsteten Kirchen zu restaurieren und neue im barocken Stil zu errichten. Doch der Zusammenbruch des spanischen Weltreichs und die Besetzung Brügges durch die Truppen von Ludwig XIV. verzögerten den Wiederaufschwung bis zur

Errichtung der österreichischen Herrschaft im Jahre 1715. Unter der Regentschaft von Kaiserin Maria-Theresa (1740-1780) und der Alleinregierung ihres Schwagers Karl von Lothringen begann eine wirtschaftliche Erholung durch den Aushub eines Hafenbeckens für Hochseeschiffe, die Schaffung neuer Industriezweige, die Mode der vor allem von den Beginen angefertigten Spitze.

Die Eroberung durch die französischen Republikaner führte neben der Zerstörung der romanischen Kirche St. Donatus zu Lethargie in Brügge, das inzwischen zur Hauptstadt des Departements Lys geworden war.

Die industrielle Revolution des 19. Jhs. berührte die Stadt kaum, was ihr die negativen Auswirkungen einer unkontrollierten Stadtentwicklung ersparte. Glücklicherweise setzte sich König Leopold II. nachdrücklich zu Gunsten des Baus des Hafens von Zeebrugge ein, durch den man an früheren Wohlstand anzuknüpfen hoffte. Doch kaum waren die Arbeiten beendet, besetzte die deutsche Armee einen Teil der Küste; Zeebrugge diente von 1914 bis 1918 als Kriegshafen. Und zweiundzwanzig Jahre später befanden sich erneut feindliche Torpedo-, Unterwasser- und Schnellboote in den Hafenanlagen. Aber mehr noch als der Aufschwung nach dem Ersten Weltkrieg erwies sich die auf den Zweiten Weltkrieg folgende Phase als entscheidend. Dank des Hafens zur Nordsee eroberte sich Brügge seinen Platz im internationalen Handel zurück.

Während dieser Zeit begannen die städtischen Behörden mit Restaurierungsmaßnahmen und der Wiederbelebung des architektonischen Erbes von Brügge. Sie mussten dabei allerdings Gebäude des zeitgenössischen Stils integrieren. Dieses Nebeneinander von Gegenwart und Vergangenheit ist nicht immer selbstverständlich, aber notwendig, um den Bedürfnissen des modernen Lebens zu entsprechen und zugleich die Erwartungen der Tausenden von Besuchern zu erfüllen, die nach Brügge kommen, um in dieser kostbaren Ruhestätte der Schönheit zu verweilen.

De zeven poorten van Brugge werden gebouwd in dezelfde periode als de gotische omwalling, op het einde van de 13de eeuw. Ze werden opgeknapt toen de grote gracht rond de stad dieper werd uitgegraven, en later werd verdubbeld. Vier ervan, waaronder de **Ezelpoort**, ontsnapten aan de vernielingen van de 18de eeuw.

De **Smedenpoort** werd gebouwd tussen 1297-1299 en heropgetrokken in 1615. Zijn twee dikke ronde torens flankeren de doorgang die, met twee bruggen, over de voormalige verdedigingsgracht loopt.

De **Gentpoort** werd volledig heropgebouwd in het begin van de 15de eeuw en is indrukwekkend door zijn massieve aspect dat nauwelijks wordt verzacht door twee torentjes met verfijnde dakbedekking. De meeste schietgaten zijn bewaard gebleven maar op het gelijkvloers zijn twee openingen aangebracht.

De twee torens van de **Kruispoort**, die dateert van dezelfde periode als de Gentpoort, zijn met elkaar verbonden door een muur met kantelen voor de verdediging van de toegang. Tegenwoordig opent de poort zich voor het autoverkeer. Boven de passage die vroeger werd verdedigd door een valhekken, bleven de groeven van de ophaalbrug bewaard.
Aan de kant van de stad *(rechterbladzijde)* moest het militaire karakter van de poort wijken voor architecturale versiering. Het klopt dat, als er gevaar dreigde, dat van buiten de stad kwam. Het is door deze Kruispoort dat Margaretha van York met haar gevolg de stad binnenreed na haar huwelijk met Karel de Verschrikkelijke in Damme op 3 juli 1468.

Les sept portes de Bruges furent construites en même temps que l'enceinte gothique, à la fin du XIIIᵉ siècle. Elles furent remaniées, notamment lorsque le grand fossé entourant la ville fut creusé plus profondément, puis doublé. Quatre d'entre elles, dont la **porte des Baudets**, ont échappé aux démolitions du XVIIIᵉ siècle.

La **Porte Maréchale** fut édifiée en 1297-1299 et reconstruite en 1615. Ses deux épaisses tours rondes flanquent la voie de passage qui, par deux ponts, surplombe l'ancien fossé défensif.

Totalement reconstruite au début du XVᵉ siècle, la **porte de Gand** impressionne par son aspect massif que n'atténuent guère deux tourelles terminées par une fine toiture. Elle a gardé la plupart de ses meurtrières mais a été pourvue de deux ouvertures au rez-de-chaussée.

Les deux tours de la **porte Sainte-Croix**, de la même époque que la porte de Gand, sont reliées l'une à l'autre par un mur crénelé permettant la défense de l'accès qui, aujourd'hui, s'ouvre à la circulation automobile. Au-dessus du passage défendu autrefois par une herse subsistent les feuillures du pont-levis.
Du côté de la ville *(page de droite)*, le caractère militaire de la porte à cédé devant l'ornementation architecturale. Il est vrai que, si danger il y avait, il venait de l'extérieur. C'est par la porte Sainte-Croix qu'en grand cortège, Marguerite d'York entra dans la ville après son mariage avec Charles le Téméraire à Damme le 3 juillet 1468.

The seven gates of Bruges were built at the same time as the Gothic walls at the end of the 13th century. They were altered later when the ditch around the city was deepened and doubled in width. Only four gates, one of which is the **Donkey Gate**, were not demolished in the 18th century.

The **Marshal's Gate** was built between 1297 and 1299 and rebuilt in 1615. The passageway with its two bridges crossing the old defensive ditch is flanked by two massive towers.

The impressive **Ghent Gate** with its massive walls barely lightened by two turrets with elegant roofs was completely rebuilt in the early 15th century. It still has most of its loopholes but now has two openings on the ground floor.

The two towers of the **Holy Cross Gate** date from the same period as the Ghent Gate and are linked by a crenellated wall defending the entrance, now open to automobiles. Above the passage once defended by a portcullis the rabbets of the drawbridge can be seen.
On the side of the town *(page right)* the military character of the gate has given way to architectural ornamentation. It is true that if there was danger it usually came from the outside. The grand procession of Margaret of York entered through the Holy Cross Gate after her marriage to Charles the Bold in Damme on July 3, 1468.

Die sieben Stadttore von Brügge wurden zur selben Zeit wie die gotische Umfassungsmauer, nämlich Ende des 13. Jhs., errichtet und in der Folge mehrmals umgebaut, insbesondere als der die Stadt umgebende große Graben tiefer ausgehoben und dann verdoppelt wurde. Vier von ihnen, darunter das **Eselstor**, entgingen den Abrissmaßnahmen im 18. Jh.

Das **Schmiedetor** wurde in den Jahren 1297-1299 erbaut und 1615 rekonstruiert. Seine beiden dicken Rundtürme flankieren den Durchgangsweg, der mittels zwei Brücken den alten Verteidigungsgraben überspannt.

Das Anfang des 15. Jhs. vollständig rekonstruierte **Genter Tor** beeindruckt durch sein mächtiges Aussehen, das die beiden Türmchen mit zierlichem Dach kaum abzumildern vermögen. Das Tor hat die Mehrzahl seiner Schießscharten bewahrt, wurde aber im Erdgeschoss mit zwei Öffnungen versehen.

Die beiden Türme des aus der selben Epoche wie das Genter Tor stammenden **Heiligkreuztores** sind durch eine mit Zinnen bewehrte Mauer miteinander verbunden, welche die Verteidigung des Zugangs ermöglichte, der heute dem Autoverkehr frei gegeben ist. Über dem ehemals durch ein Fallgitter geschützten Durchgang sind noch die Anschläge der Zugbrücke zu sehen.
Zur Stadtseite hin *(rechte Seite)* schwand durch die architektonische Ausschmückung der militärische Charakter des Tores. Denn tatsächlich kam Gefahr, wenn sie denn auftrat, stets von Außen. Durch eben dieses Heiligkreuztor zog Margareta von York nach ihrer Hochzeit mit Karl dem Kühnen in Damme am 3. Juli 1468 mit großem Gefolge ein.

Sint-Annawijk

Quartier Sint-Anna

Saint Anne District

St.-Anna Viertel

Rond 1550 lieten de boogschutters van de Sint-Sebastiaangilde – één van de belangrijkste van de stad – een nieuw huis bouwen in nog gotische stijl. Niettemin verraadt het architecturale decor van het elegante trappenhuis reeds enkele Renaissance-elementen, zoals de korfbogen en de medaillonportretten. Het **huis van de Sint-Sebastiaangilde** werd in de loop van de 17de eeuw aanzienlijk vergroot.

Vers 1550, les archers de la guilde de Saint-Sébastien – l'une des plus importantes de la ville – se firent construire une nouvelle maison dans un style encore gothique. Toutefois, le décor architectural de son élégante tour d'escalier révèle déjà quelques éléments Renaissance, tels que les arcs en anse de panier et les médaillons avec bustes. La **maison de la guilde de Saint-Sébastien** a été considérablement agrandie au cours du XVIIe siècle.

Around 1550 the archers of the Guild of Saint Sebastian, one of the most important in the city, had a new house built in the old Gothic style. Nonetheless, the architectural details of its elegant staircase turret incorporate a few Renaissance elements such as the basket-handle arches and medallions with busts. The **guild house of Saint Sebastian** was considerably enlarged during the 17th century.

Um das Jahr 1550 ließen sich die Bogenschützen der Gilde des heiligen Sebastians – eine der bedeutendsten der Stadt – ein neues Haus in noch gotischem Stil errichten. Die architektonische Ausgestaltung des eleganten Treppenturmes weist jedoch bereits einige Elemente der Renaissance auf, wie etwa die Korbbögen und die mit Büsten geschmückten Medaillons. Das **Haus der Gilde des heiligen Sebastians** wurde im Laufe des 17. Jhs. erheblich erweitert.

Rond 1938 begonnen de grote restauratiewerken aan de openbare monumenten van de stad. Pas vanaf de jaren 1970 begon men zich meer te bekommeren om de renovatie van privé-woningen. De oude gerenoveerde huizen van de **Peperstraat**, in de wijk van de Sint-Annakerk en de Jeruzalemkerk, zijn daarvan een voorbeeld.

Vers 1938 débutèrent de grands travaux de restauration des monuments publics de la ville. Ce n'est qu'à partir des années 1970 que l'on se soucia davantage de la rénovation des immeubles privés. L'ensemble des maisons anciennes rénovées de la **Peperstraat**, dans le quartier des églises Sainte-Anne et de Jérusalem, est exemplaire.

Around 1938 a vast campaign to restore the public monuments of the city began. Only from 1970 on was attention given to restoring private buildings. The renovation of a group of old houses on **Peperstraat** in the district of Saint Anne's church and the Jerusalem church is flawless.

Um das Jahr 1938 wurden große Restaurierungsarbeiten an den öffentlichen Bauwerken der Stadt in Angriff genommen. Erst ab den 1970er Jahren kümmerte man sich auch verstärkt um die Renovierung der Privatgebäude. Beispielhaft hierfür ist der Komplex alter restaurierter Häuser in der **Peperstraat**, dem Viertel mit der Kirche St. Anna und der Jerusalemkirche.

De **Jeruzalemkerk** is een klein heiligdom met slechts één hoofdbeuk en bestaat nu nog precies zoals ze tussen 1427 en 1429 werd gebouwd door de familie Adorno, afkomstig uit Genua. Paus Martinus V gaf toestemming voor het optrekken van een koepeltoren, geflankeerd door 4 torentjes. Deze opmerkelijke klokkentoren met zijn koepel moest een verwijziging zijn naar de H. Grafkerk in Jeruzalem.

Petit sanctuaire à une seule nef, l'**église de Jérusalem** demeure telle qu'elle fut édifiée entre 1427 et 1429 par la famille Adorno, originaire de Gênes. Le pape Martin V autorisa de la doter d'une tour-lanterne flanquée de quatre tourelles et surmontée d'une galerie. Cet étonnant campanile sommé d'une sphère était censé évoquer l'église du Saint-Sépulcre à Jérusalem.

A small sanctuary with a single nave, the **Jerusalem church** remains as it was originally built between 1427 and 1429 by the Adorno family from Genoa. Pope Martin V gave permission to erect a lantern tower flanked by four turrets and surmounted by a gallery. This astonishing campanile capped with a sphere was supposed to evoke the church of the Holy Sepulcher in Jerusalem.

Die kleine **Jerusalemkirche** mit nur einem Schiff zeigt sich noch so, wie sie zwischen 1427 und 1429 von der aus Genua stammenden Familie Adorno erbaut worden war. Papst Martin V. erteilte die Erlaubnis, sie mit einem von vier Türmchen flankierten und einer Galerie umgebenen Laternenturm auszustatten. Dieser erstaunliche, kugelförmig abgeschlossene Kampanile sollte an die Grabeskirche in Jerusalem erinnern.

In de Balstraat, niet ver van de Jeruzalemkerk, groepeert het **museum voor Volkskunde** een tiental lage huizen gebouwd in de 16de eeuw. Het interieur schetst de verschillende aspecten van het dagelijkse leven in Vlaanderen. In een klasje van de lagere school bevindt zich een verzameling didactisch materiaal. In de keuken werd de tafel gedekt voor de maaltijd, vlakbij de houten tobbe. In zijn atelier herstelt de kuiper één van de twee platte bodems, nadat hij de eikehouten duigen heeft geassembleerd.

Dans la Balstraat, non loin de l'église de Jérusalem, le **musée du Folklore** groupe une dizaine de maisons basses édifiées au XVIe siècle. Ses intérieurs reconstituent les différents aspects de la vie quotidienne flamande. Dans une classe d'école primaire, tout le matériel didactique se trouve réuni. Dans la cuisine, la table a été dressée pour le repas, à proximité de la cuve en bois. Dans son atelier, le tonnelier, après avoir assemblé les douves de chêne, fixe l'un des deux fonds plats.

The **Folklore Museum** in Balstraat, not far from the Jerusalem church occupies a group of ten low houses with high roofs of the 15th century. Various aspects of Flemish daily life are presented in the interior. In a primary school classroom all the educational material is shown. In the kitchen the table is set for a meal. A cooper in his workshop, having assembled the oak staves of a barrel, is installing one of the flat bottoms.

Das **volkskundliche Museum** in der Balstraat, nicht weit von der Jerusalemkirche entfernt, umfasst zehn niedrige Häuser aus dem 16. Jh. In den Innenräumen werden die verschiedenen Aspekte des flämischen Alltaglebens nachgestellt. In einem Klassenraum einer Grundschule ist alles didaktische Material zusammengetragen. In der Küche wurde in der Nähe des Holzzubers der Tisch für die Mahlzeit gedeckt. Der Böttcher befestigt in seiner Werkstatt eine der beiden platten Böden, nachdem er die Eichendauben zusammengesetzt hat.

Langerei &
Jan van Eyckplein

Langerei &
place Jan van Eyck

Langerei &
Jan van Eyck Square

Langerei &
Jan van Eyck-Platz

In de 11de eeuw verbond de Langerei het havenkwartier van de **Spiegelrei** rechtstreeks met de zee, waarin in die tijd de Reie uitmondde. Dit zorgde voor de commerciële ontwikkeling van Brugge in de Middeleeuwen. Markies Spinola, die in 1604 Oostende veroverde van Maurits van Nassau, had aan deze kant van de Spiegelrei een belangrijk verblijf, dat dan ook zijn naam droeg *(links)*.

Vlak bij de **Langerei**, waar een huis met het jaartal 1734 opvalt door zijn bijzondere barokke puntgevel en de levendige kleur van de voorgevel, ziet men de massieve bakstenen toren van de **Sint-Gilliskerk** in primitieve gotische stijl eigen aan de kuststreek en de polders van het maritieme Vlaanderen.

De houten voorgevel van het **Genthof** dateert van het einde van de 15de eeuw. In de 13de en 14de eeuw waren de meeste huizen opgetrokken uit hout en bedekt met riet. Dat was niet meer het geval in de 15de eeuw. Huizen werden toen opgetrokken in baksteen met dakpannen, maar men gebruikte nog vaak hout om de voorgevel te versieren. Op de achtergrond steekt de toren van het Oosterlingenhuis uit (14de eeuw).

De Poortersloge *(links)* werd gebouwd in de 15de eeuw vlakbij de **Spiegelrei**, ter hoogte van de voormalige Sint-Jansbrug, en diende als ontmoetingsplaats voor de bourgeoisie. De Spiegelrei *(rechts)* beschikte over een haveninstallatie en bracht een grote economische activiteit teweeg. Men loste en laadde er schepen uit alle landen van het Westen. Daarom werd in 1478 het Tolhuis gebouwd, een sierlijk gotisch bouwwerk met een voorgevel in witte steen, tegenover de Loge van de Bourgeoisie; men inde er de tolrechten op de internationale en interregionale handel. De havenarbeiders van de Sint-Jansbrug moesten vanzelfsprekend over een lokaal beschikken. Ze kregen er één in 1470, naast het Tolhuis. In het midden van het huidige **Jan van Eyckplein** staat sinds 1856 het standbeeld van de schilder.

Au XIᵉ siècle, le Langerei (le *long canal*) reliait le quartier portuaire du **Spiegelrei** directement à la mer dans laquelle s'écoulait naturellement la Reie à cette époque, ce qui permit le développement commercial de Bruges au moyen âge. Le marquis Spinola, qui en 1604 enleva Ostende à Maurice de Nassau, avait une importante demeure de ce côté du Spiegelrei qui porte désormais son nom *(à gauche)*.

Proche du **Langerei**, où une maison portant le millésime de 1734 se distingue par son curieux pignon baroque et la couleur vive de sa façade, la tour massive en brique de l'**église Saint-Gilles** appartient au style gothique primitif de la région côtière et des polders de la Flandre maritime.

La façade en bois du **Genthof** date de la fin du XVᵉ siècle. Aux XIIIᵉ et XIVᵉ siècles, la majorité des maisons étaient en bois et couvertes de chaume. Ce n'était plus le cas au XVᵉ siècle. On les construisit en brique avec toit de tuiles mais on utilisait souvent le bois pour décorer la façade. À l'arrière-plan pointe la tourelle de la Maison des Osterlins (XIVᵉ s.).

La Loge des Bourgeois *(à gauche)* fut édifiée au XVᵉ siècle près du **Spiegelrei** à hauteur de l'ancien pont Saint-Jean, afin de servir de local de réunion pour les bourgeois. Pourvu d'installations portuaires, le Spiegelrei *(à droite)* drainait une importante activité économique. On y chargeait et déchargeait des navires de tous les pays d'Occident. D'où la construction en 1478 de la maison du tonlieu, gracieux édifice gothique à la façade de pierre blanche, face à la Loge des Bourgeois; l'on y percevait les droits de douane sur le commerce international et interrégional. Les débardeurs du pont Saint-Jean devaient évidemment disposer d'un local. Ils en furent dotés en 1470, contigu à la maison du tonlieu. Au centre de l'actuelle **place Jan van Eyck** se dresse depuis 1856 la statue du peintre.

In the 11th century the Langerei (the *long canal*) linked the port district of the **Spiegelrei** directly to the sea into which the Reie flowed at that time, permitting the commercial development of Bruges during the Middle Ages. The Marquis of Spinola who took Ostend from Maurice of Nassau in 1604 had an imposing house which henceforth carried his name on this side of the Spiegelrei *(left)*.

Near the Langerei where a house bearing the date 1734 has a curious baroque gable and a brilliantly coloured façade rises the massive brick tower of **Saint Gilles' church** built in the early Gothic style of the coastal region and polders of maritime Flanders.

The wooden façade of the **Genthof** dates from the late 15th century and was restored in its original style in 1967. During the 13th and 14th centuries most houses were in wood with thatched roofs but this was not so in the 15th century. They were then built in brick with tile roofs but wood was often used to decorate the façades. In the background rises the turret of the 14th century House of the Easterlings.

The Burghers Lodge *(left)* was built in the 14th century near the **Spiegelrei** by the old Saint John's bridge for meetings of the burghers. The port installations of the Spiegelrei *(right)* generated intense economic activity, loading and unloading ships from all the western countries. This in turn led to the construction in 1478 of the graceful Gothic tollhouse with its white façade facing the Burghers Lodge. Customs duties on international and interregional commerce were collected there. The longshoremen of Saint John's bridge naturally also required a meeting place which they received in 1470, next to the tollhouse. Since 1856 a statue of the artist stands in the centre of the **Jan van Eyck square** which bears his name.

Im 11. Jh. verband der Langerei (der *lange Kanal*) das Hafenviertel des **Spiegelrei** direkt mit dem Meer, in das die Reie zu dieser Zeit mündete. Dies ermöglichte im Mittelalter den Aufbau von Handelsaktivitäten in Brügge. Markgraf Spinola, der Maurice von Nassau 1604 Ostende wegnahm, besaß eine bedeutende Wohnstätte auf dieser Seite des Spiegelrei, die nun seinen Namen trägt *(links)*.

In der Nähe des **Langerei**, wo sich das Haus mit der Jahreszahl 1734 durch seinen kuriosen barocken Giebel und die leuchtende Farbe seiner Fassade von den anderen abhebt, gehört der massive Backsteinturm der **Kirche St. Ägidius** dem primitiven gotischen Stil der Küstenregion und der Poldern des maritimen Flanderns an.

Die Holzfassade des **Genthofs** stammt aus dem Ende des 15. Jhs. Im 13. und 14. Jh. waren die meisten Häuser aus Holz gebaut und mit Stroh gedeckt. Dies änderte sich im 15. Jh. Man errichtete nun Backsteingebäude mit Ziegeldächern, verwendete aber häufig noch das Holz zur Ausschmückung der Fassade. Im Hintergrund ragt das Türmchen des Asiatenhauses (14. Jh.) empor.

Die *Poortersloge* (=Bürgerloge, *links*) wurde im 15. Jh. nahe dem **Spiegelrei** in Höhe der alten St.-Johannes-Brücke errichtet und diente den Bürgern als Versammlungsort. Der mit Hafenanlagen ausgestattete Spiegelrei *(rechts)* zog bedeutende wirtschaftliche Aktivitäten an. Schiffe aus allen westlichen Ländern wurden dort be- und entladen. Daher auch der Bau des Zollhauses im Jahre 1478, eines reizenden gotischen Gebäudes mit einer Fassade aus weißem Stein gegenüber der Bürgerloge, in dem man dann die Zollgebühren für den internationalen und zwischenregionalen Handel eintrieb. Die Hafenarbeiter der St. Johannes-Brücke mussten selbstverständlich über einen eigenen Raum verfügen. Im Jahre 1470 bekamen sie einen solchen in Angrenzung an das Zollhaus. In der Mitte des heutigen **Jan van Eyck Platzes** steht seit 1856 die Statue des Malers.

Fotografen en schilders dragen bij tot de bekendheid van de **Groenerei**, zijn ezelsbruggetjes, zijn zicht op het belfort en de klokketoren van de Onze-Lieve-Vrouwkerk. Hij is afgeboord met oude huizen waarvan de verschillende stijlen bijdragen tot de charme van het geheel. Er zijn zelfs enkele terrastuinen te vinden, met bomen waarvan de takken het rustige water beroeren.

Het Brugse Vrije, de uitgestrekte regio rond de stad, was het belangrijkste burggraafschap van Vlaanderen. Van het **Landhuis van het Brugse Vrije**, gebouwd in 1520, blijft het oudste gedeelte op het kanaal bestaan. De drie bakstenen voorgevels van de Schepenkamer (1520-1523), de *Vertrekkamer* (1522-1523) en de *Wezenkamer* zijn gelijkend maar hun puntgevels zijn verschillend. Elk van de gevels is omringd door fijne polygonale torentjes die bij hun restauratie iets werden verfraaid.
De elegante voorgevel van het huis *"De Caese" (rechts)* maakte deel uit van het Landhuis van het Vrije ; de gevel is zeer symmetrisch opgebouwd, beschilderd in een camaïeu die natuursteen imiteert, en behoort tot de Lodewijk XV-stijl.

De **schouw van het Brugse Vrije** werd gebouwd tussen 1528 en 1531 onder leiding van Lanceloot Blondeel en beslaat een volledige muur van de Schepenzaal. De schouw is opgedragen aan Karel V, winnaar van de slag in 1525. Rond de keizer bevinden zich, op ware grootte, zijn grootouders, Maximiliaan van Oostenrijk, Maria van Bourgondië, Ferdinand van Aragon en Isabella van Castilië, gemaakt door Guyot de Beaugrant.

De **Steenhouwersdijk** draagt zijn naam sinds de 14de eeuw, niet omwille van de aanwezigheid van steenhouwers maar wel als referentie aan een bekende Brugse familie aan het eind van de 13de eeuw.

Photographes et peintres et ne se lassent pas de populariser le **Groenerei**, ses ponts en dos d'âne, sa perspective sur la tour du beffroi et le clocher de Notre-Dame. Il est bordé de maisons anciennes dont l'alternance des styles ajoute au charme ambiant. Il comporte même quelques jardins en terrasse, plantés d'arbres dont les branches débordent sur les eaux dormantes.

Le Franc de Bruges, la vaste région aux alentours de cette ville, constituait la châtellenie la plus importante de Flandre. Du **palais du Franc de Bruges** construit en 1520 subsiste la partie la plus ancienne, sur le canal. Les trois façades en briques de la Chambre des échevins (1520-1523), de la *Vertrekkamer* (1522-1523) et la *Wezenkamer* sont semblables mais leurs pignons sont distincts. Chacun de ceux-ci est entouré de fines tourelles polygonales quelque peu enjolivées lors de leur restauration.
L'élégante façade de la maison *"De Caese" (à droite)* faisait partie du palais du Franc ; très symétrique, peinte en un camaïeu qui imite les pierres naturelles, elle appartient au style Louis XV.

Réalisée entre 1528 et 1531 sous la direction de Lancelot Blondeel, la **cheminée du Franc de Bruges** occupe tout un mur de la Salle des échevins. Elle est dédiée à Charles Quint vainqueur de la bataille de Pavie en 1525. Autour de l'empereur sont représentés en grandeur nature ses grands-parents, Maximilien d'Autriche, Marie de Bourgogne, Ferdinand d'Aragon et Isabelle de Castille par Guyot de Beaugrant.

La **Steenhouwersdijk** (digue des Marbriers) est ainsi appelé depuis le XIVe siècle, non pas à cause de la présence de tailleurs de pierre mais bien par référence au nom d'une famille connue à Bruges à la fin du XIIIe siècle.

Photographers and artists never tire of the **Groenerei** with its humpbacked bridge and vista of the city belfry and the belfry of Our Lady's church. It is lined with old houses whose differing styles add to its charm. It even has a few terraced gardens with trees the branches of which hang over the still waters.

The Franc, or free zone, of Bruges, a large region around the city, was the most important castellany of Flanders. Of the **administrative palace of the Franc of Bruges** there remains the oldest part built in 1520 on the canal. The three façades of the Magistrates Chamber (1520-1523), the *Vertrekkamer* (1522-23) and the *Wezenkamer* are similar except for their gables. Each house has delicate polygonal turrets, somewhat embellished during their restoration.
The elegant façade of the *"De Caese"* mansion was part of the regional palace. In the Louis XV style, it is very symmetrical and painted in monochrome, imitating stone.

The **fireplace of the Franc of Bruges**, constructed between 1528 and 1531 under the supervision of Lancelot Blondeel takes up a whole wall in the Aldermen's Chamber. It is dedicated to Charles V, victor at Pavia in 1525. Around the Emperor are life-size statues of his grandparents Maximilian of Austria, Mary of Burgundy, Ferdinand of Aragon and Isabella of Castile, sculpted by Guyot de Beaugrant.

The **Steenhouwersdijk** (stone cutters dike) was so named in the 14th century but not because of stone cutters. It refers to a Bruges family of that name, prominent at the end of the 13th century.

Fotografen und Maler werden nicht müde, den **Groenerei**, seine gewölbten Brücken und den Anblick vom Turm des Belfrieds oder dem Glockenturm der Liebfrauenkirche herab zu verewigen. Der Kanal wird von alten Häusern gesäumt, deren Stilvielfalt zum Charme der Umgebung beiträgt. Es finden sich sogar einige Terrassengärten, die mit Bäumen bepflanzt sind, deren Zweige auf das ruhige Wasser hinausragen.

Die Freigrafschaft von Brügge, die weite Region um diese Stadt herum, stellte die wichtigste Burggrafschaft von Flandern dar. Von dem im Jahre 1520 erbauten **Sitz der Brügger Freigrafschaft** existierte noch der älteste, dem Kanal zugewandte Teil. Die drei Backsteinfassaden des Schöffensaals (1520-1523), der *Vertrekkamer* (1522-1523) und der *Wezenkamer* sind gleichartig gestaltet, nur ihre Giebel unterscheiden sich voneinander. Alle sind mit zierlichen, vieleckigen Türmchen versehen, die bei der Restaurierung ein wenig ausgeschmückt wurden.
Die elegante Fassade des Hauses *"De Caese" (rechte Seite)* war Teil des Gebäudes der Freigrafschaft. Das äußerst symmetrische, in einem die Natursteine nachahmenden, tonigen Anstrich gehaltene Bauwerk gehört dem Louis-quinze an.

Der zwischen 1528 und 1531 nach Entwürfen von Lancelot Blondeel errichtete **Kamin des Sitzes der Freigrafschaft von Brügge** nimmt eine ganze Wand im Schöffensaal ein. Er ist Karl V., dem Sieger der Schlacht von Pavia im Jahre 1525, gewidmet. In der plastischen Umsetzung von Guyot de Beaugrant umgeben den Kaiser in Lebensgröße seine Großeltern, Maximilian von Österreich, Maria von Burgund, Ferdinand von Aragonien und Isabella von Kastilien.

Der **Steenhouwerdijk** (Steinmetzdeich) trägt seit dem 14. Jh. diesen Namen, der nicht auf die Präsenz von Steinhauern zurückzuführen ist, sondern auf den Namen einer Ende des 13. Jhs. bekannten Familie von Brügge Bezug nimmt.

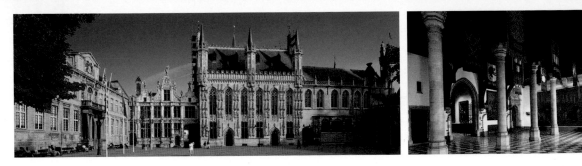

De **Blinde Ezelstraat** heeft haar naam te danken aan een herberg met dit opschrift, die verdween bij de opbouw van de Oude Griffie. Ze verbond de Burg met de Ezelsbrug op de Reie en verzekerde zo de verbinding tussen de administratieve functies en de economische activiteiten op de nabije Vismarkt.
Een sierlijk steegje in Renaissancestijl (1531-1535) werd opgetrokken tussen het stadhuis en de Oude Griffie. De achtergevel heeft kantelen vanaf het dak en de ramen dragen een decoratief kader. De voormalige "Thesaurie" van het stadhuis *(links)* is soberder en draagt het jaartal 1614. De achtergevels van deze twee gebouwen rusten op typisch Brugse kelders, met deuren en ramen die op het kanaal uitgeven.

De **Burg** is het historische hart van de stad en toont nu de opeenvolgende bijdragen van een bijna onophoudelijke architecturale evolutie. In 1134 begon graaf Diederik van den Elzas met de bouw van een kapel *(rechts)* in twee niveau's opgedragen aan Sint Basiel. Enkele jaren later werden de relieken van het Heilig Bloed neergelegd in de bovenste kapel.
Het stadhuis werd gebouwd tussen 1376 en 1421. De gotische vertikaalheid wordt niet verstoord door de nissen met standbeelden van de graven en gravinnen van Vlaanderen. De Oude Griffie (1534) leunt aan tegen het stadhuis en heeft een voorgevel in eerste Vlaamse Renaissancestijl. Het Landhuis van het Brugse Vrije (1726, *links*) getuigt van invloeden van het Franse classicisme ; het gebouw herbergt tegenwoordig de toeristische stadsdiensten.

Vier stenen zuilen ondersteunen het plafond van de **vestibule van het Stadhuis**. De vaandels herinneren aan de belangrijke rol van de ambachten in het politieke en sociale leven van Brugge. Aan de muren hangen schilderijen uit de 19de eeuw die de dood van Karel de Verschrikkelijke en Maria van Bourgondië voorstellen.

La **rue de l'Âne Aveugle** doit son nom à une auberge qui portait l'enseigne «*Den Blenden Ezel*» et disparut lors de la construction du Greffe civil. Elle reliait le Burg au pont de l'Âne sur la Reie, assurant en quelques sorte la jonction entre les fonctions administratives et les activités économiques du Marché aux Poissons tout proche.
Une gracieuse passerelle de style Renaissance (1531-1535) fut établie entre l'hôtel de ville et le Greffe civil. La façade arrière de celui-ci est crénelée au départ de la toiture et ses fenêtres comportent un encadrement décoratif. Plus dépouillée, l'ancienne «*Thesaurie*» de l'hôtel de ville *(à gauche)* porte le millésime 1614. Les façades arrière de ces deux bâtiments reposent sur des caves typiquement brugeoises, avec portes et fenêtres s'ouvrant sur le canal.

Cœur historique de la ville, le **Burg** révèle aujourd'hui dans toute leur splendeur les apports successifs d'une évolution architecturale quasi continue. En 1134, le comte Thierry d'Alsace entreprit la construction d'une chapelle à double niveau *(à droite)* dédiée à saint Basile. Quelques années plus tard, des reliques du Saint Sang furent déposées dans la chapelle supérieure.
L'hôtel de ville fut édifié de 1376 à 1421. Sa verticalité gothique n'est pas entravée par les niches des statues des comtes et comtesses de Flandre. Adossé à l'hôtel de ville, le Greffe civil (1534) présente une façade de la première Renaissance flamande. Le palais du Franc de Bruges (1726, *à gauche*) témoigne de l'influence du classicisme français ; l'édifice abrite aujourd'hui les services communaux du tourisme.

Quatre colonnes de pierre soutiennent le plafond du **vestibule de l'hôtel de ville**. Les bannières appendues rappellent le rôle primordial des métiers dans la vie politique et sociale de Bruges. Aux murs, des peintures du XIXᵉ siècle évoquent la mort de Charles le Téméraire et celle de Marie de Bourgogne.

The **street of the Blind Donkey** derives its name from an inn named "*Den Blinden Ezel*" which was demolished when the municipal registry was built. It linked the Burg to the Donkey bridge on the Reie, providing access between the administrative offices and the economic life of the nearby fish market.
A graceful Renaissance passageway (1531-35) was built from the City Hall to the registry. The rear façade of the registry has a crenellated roof and windows with decorative frames. Less ornate, the old treasury of the City Hall *(left)* bears the date 1614. The rear façades of these two buildings stand on typical Bruges cellars with doors and windows opening on the canal.

The **Burg**, the historic centre of the city, today presents in all its splendour the continuous evolution of architecture. In 1134 Count Thierry of Alsace began the construction of a two-storey chapel dedicated to Saint Basil *(right)*. A few years later the relics of the Holy Blood were placed in the upper chapel.
The City hall was built between 1376 and 1421. Niches containing statues of the Counts and Countesses of Flanders do not lessen its Gothic verticality. The Municipal registry abutting City Hall is in the early Flemish Renaissance style (1534). The palace of the Franc of Bruges (1726, *left*) testifies the influence of French neoclassicism. It is now the municipal tourist office.

Four stone columns support the ceiling of the **City Hall vestibule**. The suspended banners recall the important role of the trades and crafts in the social and political life of Bruges. The 19th century paintings on the walls recount the deaths of Charles the Bold and Mary of Burgundy.

Die **Straße des blinden Esels** verdankt ihrem Namen einem Gasthaus mit dem Schild "*Den Blenden Ezel*", das beim Bau der Zivilgerichtsschreiberei abgerissen wurde. Sie verband die Burg mit der Eselsbrücke über die Reie und sicherte so gewissermaßen die Verbindung zwischen den Verwaltungsfunktionen und den wirtschaftlichen Aktivitäten des nahen Fischmarktes.
Eine reizende Fußgängerbrücke wurde im Renaissance-Stil (1531-1535) zwischen dem Rathaus und der Zivilgerichtsschreiberei errichtet. Die rückwärtige Fassade Letzterer ist vom Dach an mit Zinnen bewehrt und die Fenster weisen eine schmückende Umrahmung auf. Das schlichtere alte "*Schatzamt*" des Rathauses *(links)* trägt die Jahreszahl 1614. Die rückwärtigen Fassaden dieser beiden Gebäude ruhen auf typischen Brügger Kellern mit Türen und Fenstern zum Kanal hin.

An der **Burg**, dem historischen Kern der Stadt, sind heute die aufeinander folgenden, beinahe kontinuierlichen architektonischen Strömungen und Entwicklungen in all ihrer Pracht sichtbar. Im Jahre 1134 ließ Graf Dietrich vom Elsass eine dem heiligen Basilius geweihte Kapelle über zwei Ebenen erbauen *(rechts)*. Einige Jahre später wurden die Reliquien des Heiligen Blutes in die obere Kapelle überführt.
Das Rathaus wurde von 1376 bis 1421 errichtet. Sein gotischer Vertikalismus wird durch die Nischen mit den Statuen der Grafen und Gräfinnen von Flandern nicht beeinträchtigt. Die an das Rathaus angelehnte Zivilgerichtsschreiberei (1534) weist eine Fassade aus der ersten flämischen Renaissance auf. Der Sitz der Freigrafschaft von Brügge (1726, links) zeugt vom Einfluss des französischen Klassizismus; das Gebäude beherbergt heute die städtischen Touristendienste.

Vier Steinsäulen stützen die Decke des **Vorraums des Rathauses**. Die dort hängenden Banner erinnern an die wichtige Rolle der Handwerker im politischen und sozialen Leben von Brügge. An den Wänden zeigen Gemälde aus dem 19. Jh. den Tod von Karl dem Kühnen und Maria von Burgund.

Tussen 1890 en 1905 werd de **gothische zaal** gereconstitueerd op basis van bestaande elementen, voornamelijk het gewelf in polychroom hout daterend uit 1402. De neogotische muurschilderingen vertellen verhalen uit de geschiedenis van Brugge. De monumentale schouw werd in 1895 geschonken door de provinciale autoriteiten.

De bovenste kapel van de **H.-Bloed-basiliek**, waar rond 1250 de relieken van het bloed van Christus werden neergelegd, werd op het einde van de 16de eeuw verbouwd.
Achter het neogotische herenhuis van J.B. Béthune – één van de actiefste protagonisten van de neogotische stijl in België – hangen schilderijen uit het begin van de 20ste eeuw die de kruisiging en diverse religieuze motieven voorstellen.

De eerste vermelding van de **Heilige Bloedprocessie** dateert van 1291. Sinds die tijd herdenken groepen vrijwilligers op Hemelvaartsdag de terugkeer van de kruisvaarder Diederik van den Elzas met een lange en spectaculaire stoet. Voor die gelegenheid haalt men het schrijn van het H. Bloed uit de basiliek. De smid Jan Crabbe maakte het schrijn tussen 1614 en 1617.

De **Proosdij van Sint-Donaas** (rechts), zetel van de rijke heren wiens domeinen zich uitstrekten over het Brugse Vrije, werd opgericht tussen 1662 en 1665, vlakbij de nu verdwenen Sint-Donaaskathedraal. De architect, Cornelis Verhouve, was een Antwerpenaar. Dat springt in het oog: de barokke stijl van dit majestueuze gebouw, waarin witte en blauwe steen elkaar afwisselen, is niet typisch Brugs maar ligt in de lijn van Pieter Paul Rubens. Op het gelijkvloers zijn de zuilen ionisch, de kantelen op de verdieping zijn corintisch van stijl. De decoratie van het portaal ontwikkelt zich vanaf het balkon in een combinatie van vrouwenfiguren, krullen en slingers.

Entre 1890 et 1905, la **salle gothique** a été reconstituée à partir d'éléments existants, en particulier la voûte en bois polychromé à pendentif de 1402. Les peintures murales néo-gothiques racontent des épisodes de l'histoire de Bruges. La cheminée monumentale a été offerte en 1895 par les autorités provinciales.

La chapelle supérieure de la **basilique du Saint-Sang**, où furent déposées vers 1250 les reliques du sang du Christ, a été remaniée à la fin du XVIe siècle.
Derrière le maître-hôtel néo-gothique de J.-B. Béthune – l'un des plus actifs protagonistes du style néo-gothique en Belgique – les peintures du début du XXe siècle représentent la crucifixion et divers motifs religieux.

La plus ancienne mention de la **procession du Saint-Sang** date de 1291. Depuis lors, le jour de l'Ascension, des groupes d'acteurs bénévoles commémorent le retour du comte-croisé Thierry d'Alsace en long et spectaculaire cortège. À cette occasion, on sort de la basilique la châsse du Saint-Sang exécutée de 1614 à 1617 par l'orfèvre Jan Crabbe.

La **Prévôté de Saint-Donatien** (à droite), siège de cette riche seigneurie dont les domaines s'étendaient sur le Franc de Bruges, fut érigée entre 1662 et 1665 à proximité de la cathédrale Saint-Donatien aujourd'hui disparue. L'architecte, Corneille Verhouve, était anversois. Cela saute aux yeux : le style baroque de ce majestueux bâtiment, où alternent pierre blanche et pierre bleue, n'est pas typiquement brugeois mais s'inscrit dans la ligne de Pierre-Paul Rubens. Ioniques au rez-de-chaussée, les chapiteaux sont corinthiens à l'étage. La décoration du portail développe à partir du balcon une combinaison de figures féminines, de volutes et de guirlandes.

Between 1890 and 1905 the **Gothic Hall** was reconstituted beginning with the existing elements such as the polychrome vaulting with pendentives of 1402. The Gothic Revival murals recount episodes in the history of Bruges. The monumental chimney-piece was donated in 1895 by the provincial government.

The upper chapel of the **Holy Blood Basilica** where relics of the blood of Christ were enshrined around 1250 was renovated at the end of the 16th century.
Behind the Gothic Revival high altar by J.B. Bethune, one of the most prolific artists in that style in Belgium, are paintings of the Crucifixion and various religious subjects from the early 20th century.

The earliest reference to the **procession of the Holy Blood** dates from 1291. Ever since then on Ascension Day groups of volunteer actors commemorate the return of Thierry of Alsace, the Crusader Count, in a long and spectacular parade. The reliquary of the Holy Blood made by the goldsmith Jan Crabbe between 1614 and 1617 is removed from the basilica and carried aloft in the procession.

The **provostship of Saint Donatien** (right), seat of the rich seigneury the domanial lands of which stretched out on the Franc of Bruges, was built from 1162 to 1665 near the Cathedral of Saint Donatien which no longer exists. That the architect Cornelius Verhouve was an Antwerper is evident in the majestic building with alternating white and blue stone, more in the style of Peter Paul Rubens than in the style of Bruges. The capitals of the columns are Ionic on the ground floor but Corinthian on the upper storey. The decoration of the portal above the balcony combines feminine faces, volutes and garlands.

Zwischen 1890 und 1905 wurde der **gotische Saal** unter Verwendung bereits vorhandener Elemente, insbesondere des polychromen Holzgewölbes mit Pendentif aus dem Jahre 1402, rekonstruiert. Die neugotischen Wandmalereien erzählen Episoden aus der Geschichte Brügges. Der riesige Kamin ist ein Geschenk der Provinzbehörden aus dem Jahre 1895.

Die obere Kapelle der **Heiligblut-Basilika**, in die man um das Jahr 1250 die Reliquien des Blutes Christi überführte, wurde Ende des 16. Jhs. umgebaut.
Die Gemälde aus dem Anfang des 20 Jhs. hinter dem neugotischen Hauptaltar von J.-B. Béthune – einem der aktivsten Vertreter des neugotischen Stils in Belgien – stellen die Kreuzigung und verschiedene religiöse Motive dar.

Die **Heiligblut-Prozession** wurde zum ersten Mal im Jahre 1291 erwähnt. Seitdem gedenken an Christi Himmelfahrt Gruppen freiwilliger Akteure mit einem langen und eindrucksvollen Prozessionszug der Rückkehr des Kreuzfahrer-Grafen Dietrich vom Elsass. Zu diesem Anlass wird der 1614 bis 1617 von Goldschmied Jan Crabbe angefertigte Schrein des Heiligenblutes aus der Basilika hinausgetragen.

Die **Propstei St. Donatus** (rechts), Sitz dieser reichen Lehnsherrschaft, deren Gebiete sich auf die Freigrafschaft von Brügge erstreckten, wurde zwischen 1662 und 1665 in der Nähe der heute nicht mehr stehenden Kathedrale St. Donatus erbaut. Die Tatsache, dass der Architekt Cornelius Verhouve aus Antwerpen kam, fällt sofort auf: Der barocke Stil des majestätischen Bauwerks in abwechelnd weißem und blauem Stein ist nicht typisch für Brügge, sondern gehört in die Reihe von Pieter-Paul Rubens. Im Erdgeschoss sind ionische Kapitelle zu sehen, im ersten Stockwerk korinthische. Der Schmuck des Portals besteht aus einer sich vom Balkon aus entfaltenden Kombination aus Frauengestalten, Voluten und Girlanden.

De stijlen van de huizen aan de **westkant van de Grote Markt** gaan harmonieus samen. Het huis "Boechoute" op de hoek van de Sint-Amandstraat *(in het midden van de foto)* bestond reeds in de 15de eeuw maar werd in de loop van de volgende eeuwen verbouwd. Op de top van de gevel geeft een gouden windwijzer de windrichting aan. Op de tegenoverliggende hoek staat het huis "Craenenburg", beroemd vanwege zijn functie als gevangenis, waar Maximiliaan van Oostenrijk werd vastgehouden na de opstand van de Bruggelingen die vreesden voor hun privileges.
In het centrum van het plein werd in 1887 het monument onthuld van de revolteleiders van 1302 tegen de Fransen en hun aanhangers, Pieter de Coninc en Jan Breydel.

Vanaf het belfort kon de torenwachter een eventuele brand opmerken aan één van de houten huizen met rieten daken.
Vanop de toren heeft men een uitzicht op de rij bouwwerken uit de 17de eeuw die de **noordkant van de Grote Markt** vormen. Al deze huizen zijn nu gewijd aan goed eten en goed drinken. Verderop verraadt de wirwar van straatjes een stad die zich in de Middeleeuwen ontwikkelde onder een demografische 'boom'.

Het **belfort** is gebouwd in het midden van de voorgevel van de hallen, zoals een stenen arm die de omgeving wijst op de macht van de stad. De bouwwerken duurden van 1282 voor de massieve basis tot 1487 voor het achthoekige gedeelte. Aan de oostkant van de Grote Markt werden in het begin van de 20de eeuw het provinciale gouvernementshuis en de post gebouwd in neo-Brugse stijl.

Le styles des maisons du **côté occidental de la Grand-Place** se marient harmonieusement. La maison «Boechoute» à l'angle de la Sint-Amandstraat *(au centre de la photo)* existait déjà au XVe siècle mais fut transformée au cours des siècles suivants. Au sommet de sa façade un cadran doré indique la direction du vent. À l'angle opposé, la maison «Craenenburg» est célèbre pour avoir été la prison où fut détenu Maximilien d'Autriche à la suite d'une révolte des Brugeois craignant pour leurs privilèges.
Au centre de la place, le monument aux meneurs des révoltes de 1302 contre les Français et leurs partisans, Pieter de Coninc et Jan Breydel, fut inauguré en 1887.

Depuis le beffroi, le guetteur pouvait déceler l'éventuel incendie de l'une ou l'autre maison de bois et à toiture de chaume.
Du haut de la tour, on a vue sur l'alignement de construction du XVIIe siècle formant le **côté nord de la Grand-Place**. Toutes sont désormais vouées au bien-manger et au bien-boire. Au-delà, le dédale des rues révèle la pérennité du tissu urbain, tel qu'il s'est développé au moyen âge sous la poussée du «boom» démographique.

Le **beffroi** se dresse au milieu de la façade des halles tel un bras de pierre signifiant aux alentours la puissance de la ville. Sa construction s'est étalée de 1282 pour la base massive à 1487 pour sa partie octogonale. Du côté oriental de la Grand-Place, le palais du Gouvernement provincial et la poste furent édifiés au début du XXe siècle en style néo-brugeois.

The various styles of the **west side of the Grand'Place** form a harmonious ensemble. The "Boechoute" house at the corner of Sint-Amandstraat *(centre of the photo)* was already there in the 15th century but was altered in the following centuries. At the top of the façade a gilded dial indicates the wind direction. On the opposite corner the "Craenenburg" mansion is famous for having been the prison where Maximilian of Austria was held following the revolt of Bruges which feared losing its privileges.
In the centre of the square is a monument dedicated in 1889 to honour Pieter de Coninc and Jan Breydel, leaders of the revolt of 1302 against the French and their supporters.

From the belfry the lookout kept watch for possible fires of the wooden, thatched roof houses.
From the top of the tower the alignment of the 17th century buildings of the **north side of the Grand'Place** can be seen. These are now dedicated to good food and good drink. Beyond, the maze of street reveals the enduring urban fabric as it developed during the population explosion of the Middle Ages.

The **belfry** rise in the centre of the façade of the covered market like a stone arm, displaying the city's power to the surrounding countryside. The construction run from the massive base begun in 1282 to the completion of the octagonal section in 1487. On the east side of the square the Provincial Government seat and the post office are built in a neo-Bruges style in the early 20th century.

Die Baustile der Häuser an der **Westseite des Großen Marktes** harmonieren gut miteinander. Das Haus "Boechoute" an der Ecke der Sint-Amandstraat *(in der Mitte des Fotos)* stand dort bereits im 15. Jh., wurde aber im Laufe der folgenden Jahrhunderte umgebaut. Auf der Spitze seiner Fassade zeigt ein goldenes Zifferblatt die Windrichtung an. In der entgegengesetzten Ecke steht das Haus "Craenenburg" berühmt dafür, als Gefängnis gedient zu haben, in welchem Maximilian von Österreich bei einem Aufstand der um ihre Privilegien fürchtenden Brügger festgehalten worden war. Das Denkmal für die Anführer der Revolten von 1302 gegen die Franzosen und ihre Anhänger Pieter de Coninc und Jan Breydel in der Mitte des Platzes wurde im Jahre 1887 eingeweiht.

Vom Belfried aus konnte der Turmwächter erkennen, ob eines der Holzhäuser mir Rietdach in Brand geraten war.
Vom Turm herab blickt man auf die Reihe der Bauwerke des 17. Jhs, welche die **Nordseite des *Große-Marktes*** bilden. Alle diese Häuser sind nun Gaumenfreuden gewidmet. Darinter zeigt das Gewirr von Straßen noch das Bild einer Stadt, die sich im Mittelalter unter dem Druck des starken Bevölkerungswachstums entwickelte.

Der **Belfried** erhebt sich einem Steinarm gleich, welcher der Umgebung die Macht der Stadt demonstriert, in der Mitte der Fassade der Tuchhallen. Die Bauzeit dauerte von 1282 für den massiven Grundbau, bis 1487 für den achteckigen Teil. Auf der Ostseite des Großen Marktes wurden Anfang des 20. Jhs. das Palais der Provinzregierung und die Post im neu-Brügger Stil errichtet.

De binnenkoer van de **Hallen** is aan de vier zijden afgesloten. Op twee zijden werden een Renaissance gaanderij ingericht. De handelaars liepen er rond en discussieerden er op regenachtige dagen ; ze waren zeer talrijk omdat ze in de tentoonstellingszalen en verkoopshallen de meest uiteenlopende koopwaar aantroffen.

Rond de achter de Grote Markt gelegen **Eiermarkt** werden mooie huizen uit de 15de tot de 17de eeuw gerestaureerd. De meest diverse stijlen komen hier vreedzaam overeen: Brugse gothiek met getande voorgevels, barok met frontons en voluten, klassiek met dakverdiepingen, zelfs minuscule boetiekjes.

In de 13de eeuw liep de **Oude Burg**, de straat die de Hallen met de Sint-Salvatorkathedraal verbindt, langs het oude gravenkasteel, de oude burcht, vandaar zijn naam. De huizen met puntgevels behielden hun verdeling in lange, smalle percelen, typisch voor de welvarende Middeleeuwse steden waar speculatie de prijzen van de gronden de hoogte injoeg. Niettemin dateren deze huizen uit zeer verschillende periodes, gaande van de 16de tot de 20ste eeuw.

De eerste Sint-Salvatorkerk werd in 1116 door een brand vernield en in 1127 vervangen door een Romaanse tempel, die aan de westkant een indrukwekkende vierkante toren draagt. Die toren was nog niet klaar toen, anderhalve eeuw later, werd begonnen met de bouw van een gotische kerk. Gelukkig beslisten de architecten om de toren te behouden en hem in hun plannen te integreren. Hierdoor vormde hij de westelijke onderbouw van het nieuwe gebouw en gaf hij een monumentaal karakter aan dat deel van de gevel. Onder de huidige bekleding blijven nog enkele sporen over van het primitieve metselwerk, dat werd uitgevoerd met een mengeling van turf en blokken natuursteen.
De **Sint-Salvatorkatedraal** werd daar opgetrokken na de vernieling in 1799 van de voormalige Sint-Donaaskatedraal, opgedragen door de Franse revolutionairen.

La cour intérieure des **Halles** est fermée sur ses quatre côtés. Sur deux d'entre eux, une galerie Renaissance a été aménagée. Les marchands y déambulaient et y discutaient, les jours de pluie ; ils étaient particulièrement nombreux parce qu'ils trouvaient dans les salles d'exposition et de vente des halles les marchandises les plus diverses.

Autour de l'**Eiermarkt**, le Marché aux Œufs derrière la Grand-Place, on a restauré de jolies maisons du XVe au XVIIIe siècles. Les styles les plus divers s'y côtoient avec bonheur : le gothique brugeois au pignon redenté, le baroque à fronton et volutes, le classique au toit mansardé, jusqu'à la minuscule boutique.

Au XIIIe siècle la rue **Oude Burg**, qui relie les Halles à la cathédrale Saint-Sauveur, longeait le vieux château comtal, *de oude burcht*. D'où son nom. Bien qu'ayant conservé la division en parcelles longues et étroites, typique des villes médiévales prospères où la spéculation renchérissait le prix des terrains, les maisons à pignons sont d'époques fort diverses. Elles s'échelonnent du XVIe au XXe siècle.

Détruite par un incendie en 1116, la première église Saint-Sauveur fut remplacée en 1127 par un sanctuaire roman doté à l'ouest d'une puissante tour carrée. Celle-ci n'était pas achevée lorsque, un siècle et demi plus tard, fut entreprise la construction d'une église gothique. Fort heureusement, ses architectes décidèrent de conserver la tour et de l'intégrer dans leurs plans. Elle devint ainsi le massif occidental du nouvel édifice et donna un caractère monumental à cette partie de la façade. Sous le revêtement de la base, il subsiste quelques traces de la maçonnerie primitive réalisée avec un mélange de tuf et de pierre de taille.
La **cathédrale Saint-Sauveur** fut élevée à ce rang après la destruction de l'ancienne cathédrale Saint-Donatien en 1799, ordonnée par les révolutionnaires français.

The inner courtyard of the **covered market** is closed on the four sides. The numerous merchants would walk and talk on rainy days in the Renaissance gallery which runs along two sides. All kinds of merchandise could be found in the exhibition and sales rooms of the market.

Around the **Eiermarkt**, the egg market behind the Grand'Place, the pretty 15th and 16th century houses have been restored. The most disparate styles coexist happily: Bruges Gothic with step gables, baroque with pediments and volutes, neoclassical with mansard roofs and even a tiny workshop.

In the 13th century **Oude Burg** street linking the market to Holy Saviour Cathedral ran along the old castle of the Count, whence its name. Even though the gabled houses are of quite different periods, running from the 16th to the 20th century, they adhere to the customary division of land into long narrow strips typical of prosperous mediaeval towns where speculation made land very expensive.

The first church of the Holy Saviour, destroyed by fire in 1116, was replaced by a Romanesque edifice with a massive square tower on the west side in 1127. It was not yet completed a century and a half later when a Gothic church was begun. Happily, the architects decided to keep the tower and integrate it into their plans. Thus it became the west face of the new structure, giving a monumental aspect to this part of the façade. Under the foundation facings there are still some vestiges of the original masonary made in a mixture of limestone and dressed stone.
The church became **Holy Saviour Cathedral** after the destruction of Saint Donatian's Cathedral by the French in 1799.

Der Innenhof der **Tuchhallen** ist auf allen vier Seiten geschlossen. Zwei von ihnen wurden mit einer Galerie im Renaissance-Stil versehen. Dort gingen die Kaufleute bei Regentagen auf und ab und diskutierten miteinander; sie kamen in besonders großer Zahl hier her, da sie in den Ausstellungs- und Verkaufsräumen der Hallen die vielfältigsten Waren angeboten fanden.

Die hübschen Häuser aus dem 15. bis 18. Jh. rund um den **Eiermarkt** hinter dem Großen Markt wurden restauriert. Hier treffen die verschiedensten Stile gelungen aufeinander: Brügger Gotik im Pass-Giebel, Barock im Giebeldreieck und den Voluten, Klassizismus im ausgebauten Dach bis hin zu dem winzigen Geschäftsraum.

Im 13. Jh. befand sich in der **Oude Burg** Straße, welche die Hallen mit der Salvatorkathedrale verbindet, die alte Grafenburg, daher der Name. Wenn die Giebelhäuser auch die Einteilung in lange und schmale Parzellen bewahrt haben, die typisch für die blühenden mittelalterlichen Städte war, in denen die Spekulation die Grundstückspreise in die Höhe trieb, so stammen sie doch aus ganz unterschiedlichen Epochen, nämlich aus dem 16. bis 20. Jh.

Die bei einem Brand im Jahre 1116 zerstörte erste Kirche St. Salvator wurde 1127 durch ein romanisches Gotteshaus ersetzt, an dessen Westseite ein mächtiger rechteckiger Turm stehen sollte. Dieser war noch nicht ganz vollendet, als man eineinhalb Jahrhunderte später mit dem Bau einer gotischen Kirche begann. Glücklicherweise beschlossen die Architekten, den Turm zu erhalten und in ihre Pläne einzubeziehen. So wurde er zum Basiselement des westlichen Fassadenabschnitts des neuen Gebäudes und verlieh diesem einen monumentalen Charakter. Unter der Grundschicht existieren noch einige Spuren des ursprünglichen, aus einer Mischung aus Tuff und behauenem Bruchstein geschaffenen Mauerwerks. Nach der von den französischen Revolutionären befohlenen Zerstörung der alten Kathedrale St. Donatius im Jahre 1799 wurde die Kirche dann zur **Kathedrale St. Salvator** erhoben.

Vanaf het belfort kan men het mooie stadsgezicht bewonderen van de Rozenhoedkaai en zijn oude huizen met getande puntgevels. Twee ervan hebben hun torentje bewaard: links het Huidevettershuis (1630), rechts het huis Malvenda, van het eind van de 15de eeuw.
De kuip van de kaai situeert zich op de grens van het historische hart van Brugge.

Vóór 1745 was de Rozenhoedkaai de Zoutkaai. Hij kreeg zijn nieuwe naam toen er winkeltjes werden opgetrokken waar de fabrikanten van rozenkransen hun vrome waar verkochten. De kaaimuur werd hersteld, waardoor een soort van kuip ontstond waarlangs het mooie **Huidevettershuis** en zijn torentje staan (*in het midden van de foto*).
Het hotel "*Duc de Bourgogne*" (*links*), op het kleine Huidevettersplein, geniet het voorrecht twee gevels langs de Reie te hebben. Eén ervan werd voorzien van een vooruitstekend gedeelte tot in de kuip van de Rozenhoedkaai.

Tegenover de **Rozenhoedkaai** loopt de Reie langs het hotel "Het Bourgoensche Kruis" met een dubbele houten gevel, een charmante imitatie (1932) van de middeleeuwse architectuur. Langs het belangrijke huis waar in de 16de eeuw de Spaanse handelaar Juan Perez de Malvenda woonde buigt ze af in de richting van de Dyver en de O.-L.-Vrouwkerk. Met de bouw van de 122 meter hoge kerktoren, die volledig in baksteen in opgetrokken, werd begonnen rond 1270; de voltooiing volgde pas een halve eeuw later.
De **Nepomucenusbrug** (*links*) – zijn standbeeld op de reling is een reproductie van het beeld van Pieter Pepers in 1767 – volgde op een bouwwerk uit de 14de eeuw. De Reie volgde toen de eerste omwalling van de stad. Onder de bruggen kwam de bourgeoisie vaak samen in een poging ernstige conflicten te regelen zonder beroep te doen op magistraten.

Depuis le beffroi, on peut admirer le bel ensemble urbain du Quai du Rosaire et ses vieilles maisons aux pignons redentés. Deux d'entre elles ont conservé leur tourelle : à gauche, la maison des Tanneurs (1630), à droite la maison de Malvenda, de la fin du XVe siècle.
Le bassin du Quai se situe à la limite du cœur historique de Bruges.

Avant 1745, le quai du Rosaire était le quai au Sel. Il prit sa nouvelle dénomination à partir de l'installation d'échoppes où les fabricants de chapelets vendaient leur pieuse marchandise. Le mur du quai a été rétabli, créant une manière de bassin que bordent la jolie **maison des Tanneurs** et sa tourelle (*au centre de la photo*).
L'hôtel «Le duc de Bourgogne» (*à gauche*), implanté sur la petite Huidevettersplein (place des Tanneurs), a le privilège d'avoir deux façades bordant la Reie. L'une d'elles fut dotée d'une proue s'avançant dans le bassin du Quai du Rosaire.

Face au **Quai du Rosaire**, le Reie longe l'hôtel «*Het Bourgoensche Kruis*» à double façade de bois, charmant pastiche (1932) de l'architecture médiévale. Puis, longeant l'importante maison où résida au XVIe siècle le marchand espagnol Juan Perez de Malvenda, elle oblique en direction du Dijver et de l'église Notre-Dame. Entièrement bâtie en brique, la tour de l'église fut commencée vers 1270 et achevée environ un demi-siècle plus tard ; elle se dresse jusqu'à 122 mètres de hauteur.
Le **pont Saint-Jean Népomucène** (*à gauche*) – sa statue, sur le parapet, reproduit celle sculptée par Pieter Pepers en 1767 – succéda à un ouvrage construit au XIVe siècle à cet endroit. La Reie suivait alors la première enceinte de la ville. Se tenaient souvent, sur les ponts, les réunions des bourgeois qui tentaient de traiter de graves conflits sans recourir aux magistrats.

From the belfry one can admire the handsome urban grouping of the Rosary Quay and the old step-gabled houses. Two of them still have their turrets: to the left the Tanners House (1630) and to the right the Malvenda House of the late 15th century.
The basin of the quay is the edge of the historic centre of Bruges.

Until 1745 Rosary Quay was known as the salt quay. It got its new name when rosary makers set up their workshops where they sold their pious wares. The wall of the quay has been rebuilt, making a sort of basin where the pretty **house of the tanners** with its turret stands (*centre of the photo*).
The hotel "*Le duc de Bourgogne*" (*left*) standing on the small Huidevettersplein (Tanner's square) has the privilege of two façades on the Reie. One of them has a prow advancing into the basin of Rosary Quay.

Opposite the **Rosary Quay** the Reie flows in front of the hotel "*Het Bourgoensche Kruis*", a charming 1932 pastiche of mediaeval architecture. It then flows past the imposing mansion where the Spanish merchant Juan Perez de Malvenda dwelt in the 16th century, then turning towards the Dyver and the church of Our Lady. Construction of its completely brick tower began around 1270 and was finished a half century later, rising to 122 meters.
The bridge of **Saint John Nepomuk** (*left*) bearing a statue which is a replica of the one carved by Pieter Pepers in 1767 replaces a 14th century bridge on this site when the Reie followed the first walls of the city. Burghers often met on the bridges to try to settle conflicts without involving the magistrates.

Vom Belfried herab lässt sich der schöne Stadtkomplex des Rosenkranzkais und seine alten Häuser mit Pass-Giebeln bewundern. Zwei von ihnen besitzen noch ihr Türmchen: links das Haus der Gerber (1630), rechts das Haus Malvenda aus dem Ende des 15. Jhs.
Das Kaibecken befindet sich am äußeren Rand des historischen Zentrums von Brügge.

Der Rosenkranzkai hieß vor 1745 Salzkai. Seine neue Bezeichnung erhielt er, als dort Buden aufgestellt wurden, in denen die Hersteller von Rosenkränzen ihre 'fromme Ware' verkauften. Die Kaimauer wurde erneuert und bildet seitdem eine Art Becken, an welchem sich das hübsche **Haus der Gerber** mit seinem Türmchen befindet (*in der Mitte des Fotos*).
Das auf dem kleinen Huidevettersplein (Gerberplatz) stehende Gasthaus "*Duc de Bourgogne*" (*links*) hat das Privileg, zwei auf die Reie weisende Fassaden zu besitzen. Eine der beiden wurde mit einem Bug versehen, der in das Becken des Rosenkranzkais hineinragt.

Gegenüber dem **Rosenkranzkai** fließt die Reie an dem Patrizierhaus "*Het Bourgoensche Kruis*" mit doppelter Holzfassade, einer hübschen Nachahmung (1932) der mittelalterlichen Architektur, vorbei. Im Weiteren verläuft sie längs des großen Hauses, in dem im 16. Jh. der spanische Kaufmann Juan Perez de Malvenda gewohnt hatte, und biegt dann in Richtung Dyver und Liebfrauenkirche ab. Der Bau des vollständig aus Backstein bestehenden Kirchturms wurde um das Jahr 1270 begonnen und etwa ein halbes Jahrhundert später beendet. Der Turm ist 122 Meter hoch.
Die **Nepomucenusbrügge** (*links*) – die Statue des Heiligen auf der Brüstung bildet das von Pieter Pepers im Jahre 1767 geschaffene Standbild nach – trat an die Stelle eines am selben Platz im 14. Jh. errichteten Bauwerks. Die Reie folgte damals der ersten Umfassungsmauer der Stadt. Auf den Brücken fanden oft die Versammlungen der Bürger statt, die sich bemühten, ernsthafte Konflikte ohne Hilfe der Magistrate zu lösen.

Gruuthusemuseum & O.-L.-Vrouwkerk

Musée Gruuthuse & église Notre-Dame

Gruuthuse Museum & Church of Our Lady

Gruuthuse-Museum & Liebfrauenkirche

Een deel van de Reie, tussen het Gruuthusepaleis en de Rozenhoedkaai, draagt de zeer oude naam **Dyver**, wat zou betekenen "heilig water" in het Keltisch. Waarschijnlijk bevond zich hier een heidense cultusplaats.
Aan de Dyver volgde de Reie de eerste omwalling rond Brugge (begin 12de eeuw), die eerst uit hout, later uit steen werd gemaakt. Sommige delen van de rivier volgden de natuurlijke loop van het water, zoals aan de Dyver of aan de Groenerei, terwijl andere reeds tijdens de Middeleeuwen door de mens werden uitgegraven, waardoor de Reie werd afgeleid om de nieuwe wijken te beschermen tegen aanvallen.
Nu zijn het enkel nog de motorbootjes met verrukte toeristen aan boord die tijdens het hoogseizoen het water in beroering brengen.

Une partie de la Reie, entre le palais de Gruuthuse et le quai du Rosaire, porte le nom fort ancien de **Dijver** qui signifierait «eau sacrée» en langue celtique. Sans doute se trouvait-il à cet endroit un lieu de culte païen.
La Reie suivait au Dijver le contour de la première enceinte de Bruges (début XIIᵉ s.) édifiée d'abord en bois puis en pierre. Certaines parties du cours de la rivière étaient naturelles, comme au Dyver ou au Groenerei, tandis que d'autres furent dès le haut moyen âge creusées par l'homme et la Reie détournée, afin de protéger les quartiers nouvellement construits contre les agressions.
Désormais, seuls les canots à moteur chargés de touristes émerveillés sillonnent les canaux pendant la belle saison.

Part of the Reie, between the Gruuthuse mansion and Rosary Quay, retains its ancient name of **Dyver** which meant "sacred waters" in the Celtic language. Undoubtedly this was the site of a pagan cult.
At the Dyver the Reie followed the contours of the first walls of Bruges of the early 12th century, first made of wood and then in stone. Some parts of the river's course were natural such as the Dyver and the Groenerei while other courses from the late Middle Age on were man-made, diverting the Reie to protect new neighbourhoods from aggression.
Nowadays only motor boats laden with admiring visitors voyage on the canals during the tourist season.

Der Abschnitt der Reie zwischen dem Gruuthuse Palais und dem Rosenkranzkai trägt den sehr alten Namen **Dyver**, was in der keltischen Sprache wohl soviel wie "heiliges Wasser" bedeutet. Zweifelsohne befand sich an dieser Stelle eine heidnische Kultstätte.
Die Reie folgte am Dyver dem Verlauf der ersten Stadtmauer von Brügge (Anfang 12. Jh.), die zunächst aus Holz, dann aus Stein errichtet worden war. Einige Strecken des Flusslaufes hatte die Natur erschaffen wie etwa am Dyver oder am Groenerei, während andere bereits im frühen Mittelalter vom Menschen gegraben wurden, um durch Umleitung der Reie die neu entstandenen Stadtviertel gegen Angriffe zu schützen.
Heutzutage befahren nur noch Motorboote mit entzückten Touristen an Bord während der Sommermonate die Kanäle.

De familie van der Aa had haar aanzienlijke fortuin te danken aan haar monopolie op de verkoop van gruut, gefermenteerde gerst voor het brouwen van bier. Zij adopteerden de naam van hun huis. Rond 1425 begon Jan van Gruuthuse langs de Reie, waarschijnlijk op de plaats van de oude gruutopslagplaats, met de bouw van een herenhuis dat zijn zoon Lodewijk, ridder van het Gulden Vlies, aanzienlijk verhoogde.
De huidige **Arentstuin** maakte deel uit van het domein van de familie Gruuthuse. Hij wordt trouwens begrensd door een zijgevel van het paleis, met rondelen die prachtig zijn versierd met driepasbogen *(links)*. Langs de Dyver is het Arentshuis *(rechterbladzijde)* nu het Brangwynmuseum, genoemd naar de Engelse kunstenaar die in Brugge woonde tot aan zijn dood in 1956. Het museum beschikt over een verzameling schilderijen, etsen en tekeningen van hem.

Les van der Aa devaient leur fortune considérable au monopole de la vente de la *gruut*, l'orge fermenté destiné au brassage de la bière. Ils prirent le nom de leur maison. Vers 1425, Jean de Gruuthuse commença le long de la Reie, sans doute à l'emplacement de l'ancien entrepôt de *gruut*, l'édification d'une demeure seigneuriale que son fils Louis, chevalier de la Toison d'Or, augmenta considérablement.
L'actuel **jardin Arents** faisait partie du domaine des Gruuthuse. Il est d'ailleurs limité par une façade latérale du palais, aux pignons admirablement décorés d'arcs trilobés *(à gauche)*. Le long du Dyver, la maison Arents *(page de droite)* est désormais le musée Brangwyn. Du nom de cet artiste anglais qui vécut à Bruges jusqu'à sa mort en 1956, dont le musée conserve la collection de tableaux, eaux-fortes et dessins.

The van der Aa family owed its considerable fortune to the monopoly it held on the sale of *gruut*, fermented barley for making beer. They later took the name of their house, Gruuthuse as their family name. Around 1425 John of Gruuthuse began to build a lordly mansion on what was most likely the site of the old *gruut* storehouse, later considerably enlarged by his son Louis, a Knight of the Golden Fleece.
The present **Arents garden** was part of the property of the Gruuuthuse family. It is bordered by the side façade of the mansion with its handsome gable decorated with trefoil arcades *(page left)*. Along the Dyver the Arents house *(page right)* is now the Brangwyn museum named after an English artist who lived in Bruges from his birth in 1867 until his death in 1956. The museum has a collection of his drawings, engravings and paintings.

Die Familie van der Aa verdankte ihr beachtliches Vermögen dem Monopol auf den Verkauf von *gruut*, zum Bierbrauen benötigter gegorener Gerste. Sie nahmen den Namen ihres Hauses an. Um 1425 begann Jan van Gruuthuse wohl an der Stelle des alten *gruut*-Geschäftes am Ufer der Reie mit dem Bau eines herrschaftlichen Wohnsitzes, den sein Sohn Lodewijk, Ritter des Goldenen Vlies, dann erheblich erweiterte.
Der heutige **Arentsgarten** war Teil des Gutes der Familie Gruuthuse. Er wird von einer Seitenfassade des Palais mit durch Kleeblattbögen wunderschön verzierten Giebeln begrenzt *(links)*. Entlang des Dyver beherbergt das Haus Arents *(rechte Seite)* nun das Brangwyn Museum. Das nach dem bis zu seinem Tod 1956 in Brügge beheimateten englischen Künstler benannte Museum zeigt eine Sammlung seiner Gemälde, Radierungen und Zeichnungen.

Men weet niets over de eerste O.-L.-Vrouwkerk die op het eind van de 9de eeuw werd gebouwd, en ook niet over het romaanse bouwwerk dat erop volgde. Met de bouw van de huidige kerk werd begonnen tijdens het tweede kwartaal van de 13de eeuw. De stijl was toen skaldisch. Enkele jaren later liet de invloed van de Franse gothiek zich voelen in de steunbogen van de **abside van de Onze-Lieve-Vrouwkerk.**

On ne sait rien de la première église Notre-Dame fondée à la fin du IXᵉ siècle, ni guère davantage de l'édifice roman qui l'a suivie. La construction de l'actuelle église débuta durant le second quart du XIIIᵉ siècle. Son style était alors du type scaldéen. Quelques années plus tard, l'influence du gothique français se fit sentir par les arcs-boutant du **chevet de l'église Notre-Dame**.

Nothing is known of the first church of Our Lady founded in the 9th century and not much more of the Romanesque structure that replaced it. Construction of the present church began in the second quarter of the 13th century in the Scheldt style. A few years later it was influenced by the French Gothic style as may be seen in the buttresses of the **apse of the church of Our Lady**.

Über die erste, Ende des 9. Jhs. gegründete Liebfrauenkirche ist nichts bekannt und auch über das anschließende romanische Bauwerk wissen wir nicht viel. Die Arbeiten an der heutigen Kirche begannen im zweiten Viertel des 13. Jhs. in skaldischem Stil. Einige Jahre später wurde der Einfluss der französischen Gotik in den Strebebögen der **Apsis der Liebfrauenkirche** sichtbar.

Michelangelo was een beginnend beeldhouwer toen de Brugse handelaar Jan Mouscroen in 1506 zijn **Maagd met het Kind** kocht en het schonk aan de Onze-Lieve-Vrouwkerk. In de kapel van de Maagd, benadrukt de zwarte nis het witte marmer van het beeld dat een ontroerende tederheid uitstraalt.

Tegen de noordflank van de toren van de Onze-Lieve-Vrouwkerk is de **"Paradijspoort"** een doopkapel geworden. De flamboyante Brabantse gotische stijl toont een reeks boogjes die door elkaar heen lopen rond de ramen en de fijne pilasters, die reiken tot de opengewerkte balustrade, waardoor het dak aan het oog wordt onttrokken. Achteraan duidt de dubbele toren van het Gruuthusepaleis op de welgesteldheid van zijn heren. Deze torens konden indien nodig dienst doen als observatiepost.

Aan Lodewijk van Gruuthuse, die op zijn blazoen het devies *"Plus est en vous"* droeg, schrijft men het initiatief toe voor de bouw van de belangrijkste gevel van het **Gruuthusepaleis**, geflankeerd door een toren met een dubbele schacht. De gotische vertikaalheid geeft het gebouw een zeker ritme, maar de harmonie van de versiering kondigt de Renaissance aan. Het portaal is van hetzelfde type als dat van het stadhuis.

Sinds 1900 herbergt het Gruuthusepaleis de collecties van het Museum voor Archeologie en Kunstambachten. Meesterwerken van de schilder- en beeldhouwkunst gaan er samen met objecten uit het dagelijkse leven. Een enorme schouw domineert de **keuken van het Gruuthusepaleis** (15de eeuw) waarin potten en pannen en verscheidene gebruiksvoorwerpen te vinden zijn, waaronder een wafelijzer met het wapen van Bourgondië.

Michel-Ange était au début de sa carrière de sculpteur lorsque le marchand brugeois Jean Mouscroen acquit la **Vierge à l'Enfant** en 1506, pour l'offrir ensuite à l'église Notre-Dame. En la chapelle de la Vierge, le niche noire souligne la blancheur du marbre de la statue qui exprime une émouvante tendresse.

Contre le flanc nord de la tour l'église Notre-Dame, le «**portail du Paradis**» est devenu un baptistère. Son style gothique brabançon flamboyant déploie des arcatures entrecroisées autour des fenêtres et des fins pilastres, qui montent jusqu'à la balustrade ajourée dissimulant la base du toit.
À l'arrière-plan, la double tourelle du palais Gruuthuse proclame l'opulence de ses seigneurs. Elles pouvaient, en cas de nécessité, servir de poste d'observation.

C'est à Louis de Gruuthuse, qui avait attribué à son blason la devise «*Plus est en vous*», qu'il faut attribuer l'initiative de la construction de la façade principale du **palais Gruuthuse**, flanquée d'une tourelle à double corps. La verticalité gothique rythme l'édifice, mais l'harmonie de la décoration annonce la Renaissance. Le portail est du même type que celui de l'hôtel de ville.

Depuis 1900, le palais Gruuthuse abrite les collections du Musée d'archéologie et des métiers d'art. Des chefs-d'œuvre de la peinture et de la sculpture y voisinent avec les objets de la vie quotidienne. Une immense cheminée domine la **cuisine du palais Gruuthuse** (XVe siècle) où abondent marmites, chaudrons et ustensiles variés, notamment des fers à gaufres aux armes de Bourgogne.

Michaelangelo was just beginning his career as a sculptor when the Bruges merchant Jan Mouscroen bought the **Virgin with Child** in 1506, subsequently donating it to the church of Our Lady. The black niche in the Lady Chapel sets off the white marble of the statue which expresses a touching tenderness.

On the north side of the tower of Our Lady's church the **Paradise Portal** has become a baptistery. Its Brabant Flamboyant Gothic uses interwoven blind arcades around the windows and the narrow pilasters rising to a balustrade hiding the base of the roof.
In the background the double turret of the Gruuthuse mansion flaunts the opulence of its lords. It could also be used as an observation post, if needs be.

Louis of Gruuthuse who added the motto "There is more in you" to his blazon was responsible for the construction of the main façade of the **Gruuthuse mansion** flanked by a double turret. Gothic verticality sets the rhythm of the building but the harmony of the decoration announces the Renaissance. The portal is similar to that of City Hall.

Since 1900 the Gruuthuse mansion has housed the collections of the Museum of Archaeology and Arts and Crafts. Masterpieces of painting and sculpture are displayed along with objects of everyday life. An enormous fireplace dominates the **kitchen of the Gruuthuse mansion** (15th century) with its numerous pots, cauldrons and various utensils; of interest are the waffle irons with the arms of Burgundy.

Michelangelo stand noch am Anfang seiner Laufbahn als Bildhauer, als der Brügger Kaufmann Jan Mouscroen die **Jungfrau mit dem Kind** im Jahre 1506 erwarb und diese dann der Liebfrauenkirche stiftete. Die schwarze Nische in der Jungfrauenkappelle hebt die weiße Farbe des Marmors dieser Statue hervor, die eine bewegende Zärtlichkeit ausdrückt.

Das gegen die Nordseite des Turms der Liebfrauenkirche gelehnte **"Paradiesportal"** ist zu einer Taufkapelle umfunktioniert worden. Der brabantisch-spätgotische Stil wird in den sich kreuzenden Arkaturen rund um die Fenster und die schmalen Pilaster sichtbar, die bis zur durchbrochenen Balustrade reichen, welche die Dachgrundfläche verdeckt. Im Hintergrund kündet der doppelte Turm des Gruuthuse Palais vom großen Reichtum der Hausherren. Er konnte bei Bedarf als Beobachtungsposten dienen.

Die Initiative zum Bau der von einem Turm mit doppeltem Körper flankierten Hauptfassade des **Gruuthuse Palais** ging wohl von Lodewijk van Gruuthuse aus, der in sein Wappen den Spruch *"Plus est en vous"* ("In Euch ist mehr") hatte hinzufügen lassen. Die gotische Vertikalität prägt das Gebäude, doch die Harmonie der Ausschmückung kündet bereits von der Renaissance. Das Portal gleicht in seiner Bauweise dem des Rathauses.

Seit 1900 beherbergt das Gruuthuse Palais die Sammlungen des Museums für Archäologie und Kunsthandwerk. Meisterwerke der Malerei und der Bildhauerei finden sich neben Gegenständen des täglichen Lebens. Ein riesiger Kamin dominiert die **Küche des Gruuthuse Palais** (15. Jh.), in der eine Vielzahl von Kochtöpfen, Kesseln und verschiedenen Utensilien, insbesondere Waffeleisen mit dem burgundischen Wappen, vorhanden ist.

Het **Sint-Janshospitaal** werd gesticht in de 12de eeuw en onthaalde alle zieken, behalve besmettelijke. Pelgrims en reizigers vonden er regelmatig een onderkomen. Het grote gebouw werd aan de rand van de stad gebouwd, langs de Reie, omdat water noodzakelijk was. Achter de gevel die langs het kanaal loopt bevindt zich de ziekenzaal van de 14de eeuw en het religieuzenklooster (1539). Eén van de armen van de Reie loopt nog steeds onder het gebouw door, hij irrigeerde destijds de binnenkoer waar een wasplaats en een drinkplaats waren ondergebracht. Het domein beschikte ook over schuren, stallen, een bakkerij en een brouwerij. In de 16de eeuw werd de grond bewerkt, onder andere voor het kweken van medicinale planten, en een boomgaard verschafte fruit aan de zieken en de religieuzen.

In 1978 verlieten de ziekenhuisdiensten dit gebouw, dat niet langer voldeed aan de eisen van de moderne geneeskunde. Het Sint-Janshospitaal werd toen een museum en een cultureel centrum, dankzij het prestigieuze artistieke patrimonium dat er in de loop der eeuwen was opgebouwd. Men betreedt het **Memlingmuseum** via een gothische ingang die uitkomt op de binnenkoer.

De **apotheek van het Sint-Janshospitaal** dateert voornamelijk van de 17de eeuw. De versiering van de lange centrale toonbank is een typische barokstijl. Op de legplanken en in de verschillende kasten werden de traditionele medicijnen bewaard, evenals de geneeskrachtige kruiden en de zalven. De *Gratia Dei* diende voor het drogen van wonden, de *Divinum* voor het uitdrogen van de likdoorns op de voeten van de pelgrims…

Het Sint-Janshospitaal was een liefdadigheidsinstelling, gecreëerd onder impuls van de rijke bourgeoisie. Van bij de aanvang werd het hospitaal onderworpen aan de stadsautoriteiten, vertegenwoordigd door twee voogden gekozen uit de meest edelmoedige notabelen. Hun portretten versieren de **Voogdenkamer**, een salon waar de apothekers zich in vroeger tijden kwamen ontspannen in een decor van pure Vlaamse barok.

Fondé au XIIe siècle, l'**hôpital Saint-Jean** accueillait tous les malades sauf les contagieux. Les pèlerins et les voyageurs y trouvaient également refuge. Très vaste, il fut construit à la lisière de la ville, au bord de la Reie parce que l'eau était indispensable à l'établissement. Derrière la façade arrosée par le canal se trouvent la salle des malades du XIVe siècle et le couvent des religieuses (1539). Un des bras de la Reie coule encore sous le bâtiment ; il irriguait jadis la cour intérieure où un lavoir et un abreuvoir avaient été installés. Le domaine comportait aussi des granges, des étables, la boulangerie et la brasserie. Au XVIe siècle, outre un jardin de plantes médicinales, des terrains étaient cultivés et un verger fournissait des fruits aux malades et aux religieuses.

En 1978, les services hospitaliers quittèrent les lieux qui ne convenaient plus aux techniques médicales modernes. L'hôpital Saint-Jean prit alors comme destinations celles de musée et centre culturel, auxquelles le destinait son prestigieux patrimoine artistique accumulé au cours des siècles. On accède au **musée Memling** par une entrée gothique qui débouche dans la cour intérieure.

La **pharmacie de l'hôpital Saint-Jean** date principalement du XVIIe siècle. La décoration du large comptoir central est typiquement baroque. Sur les étagères et dans les différentes armoires étaient conservés les remèdes traditionnels, les herbes médicinales et les onguents. Le *Gratia Dei* servait à assécher les plaies, le *Divinum* à assécher les cors aux pieds des pèlerins…

Institution de bienfaisance créée sous l'impulsion de riches bourgeois, l'hôpital Saint-Jean fut dès ses origines soumis à l'autorité urbaine, représentée par deux tuteurs choisis parmi les notables les plus généreux. Leurs portraits ornent la **Chambre des Tuteurs**, un salon où les apothicaires venaient jadis se détendre dans un décor du plus pur style baroque flamand.

The **Hospital of Saint John** cared for all the sick except those with contagious diseases. Pilgrims and travellers also found shelter there. The huge building was erected on the edge of the city near the Reie because of the need for water. Behind the canal façade the 14th century sick ward and the nuns' convent (1539) can be seen. One of the arms of the Reie still flows under the building; it supplied water to the inner courtyard where a laundry and watering trough were installed. The domain also had barns, stables, a bakery and a brewery. In the 16th century as well as a garden of medicinal plants the land was cultivated and there was an orchard providing fruit for the nuns and the patients.

In 1978 medical services were removed from the hospital which no longer met modern medical requirements. Saint John's hospital then took on a new function as a museum and cultural centre, ordained by its rich artistic holdings accumulated over the centuries. The **Memling Museum** is reached by a Gothic entrance giving on the inner courtyard.

The **pharmacy of Saint John's hospital** dates mainly from the 16th century. The ornamentation of the large central counter is typically baroque. Traditional remedies, medicinal herbs and salves were kept on the shelves and in various cupboards. The *Gratia Dei* was used to heal wounds, the *Divinum* to relieve the corns on the feet of pilgrims…

From its inception Saint John's hospital, a charitable organization founded by wealthy burghers, was controlled by the urban authorities represented by two guardians chosen from among the most generous donors. Their portraits hang in the **Guardians Chamber** where the apothecaries used to relax amid the purest Flemish baroque decor.

Das im 12. Jh. gegründete **St. Johannes-Hospital** nahm alle Kranken mit Ausnahme von Patienten mit ansteckenden Krankheiten auf. Pilger und Reisende fanden dort ebenfalls Unterkunft. Es wurde als sehr weitläufiges Gebäude am Rande der Stadt am Ufer der Reie erbaut, da Wasser für die Einrichtung unentbehrlich war. Hinter der vom Kanal bewässerten Fassade befindet sich der Saal der Kranken aus dem 14. Jh. und das Kloster der Nonnen (1539). Einer der Arme der Reie verläuft noch unter dem Gebäude; er bewässerte einst den Innenhof, in welchem ein Waschtrog und eine Tränke aufgestellt waren. Das Gut umfasste zudem Scheunen, Ställe, eine Bäckerei und eine Brauerei. Im 16. Jh. wurde neben einem Garten mit Heilpflanzen auch das Land bestellt und ein Obstgarten lieferte den Kranken und den Nonnen frische Früchte.

1978 stellte man die Krankenhausdienste ein, da die Räumlichkeiten nicht mehr für die modernen medizinischen Techniken geeignet waren. Das St. Johannes-Hospital wurde zum Museum und Kulturzentrum, eine Bestimmung, für die es aufgrund seines kostbaren, im Laufe der Jahrhunderte gesammelten Kunstbestandes prädestiniert war. Der Zugang zum **Memling Museum** erfolgt durch einen in den Innenhof führenden gotischen Eingang.

Die **Apotheke des St. Johannes-Hospitals** stammt überwiegend aus dem 17. Jh. Die Ausstattung des breiten zentralen Ladentisches ist typisch barock. In den Regalen und diversen Schränken wurden die traditionellen Arzneien, die Heilkräuter und die Salben aufbewahrt. Das *Gratia Dei* diente zum Trocknen von Wunden, das *Divinum* zum Trocknen der Hühneraugen an den Füßen der Pilger…

Das St. Johannes-Hospital, das als Wohltätigkeitseinrichtung auf Veranlassung reicher Bürger gegründet worden war, unterstand von Anfang an der Stadtmacht, die von zwei aus den Reihen der großzügigsten Notabeln ausgewählten Vormündern repräsentiert wurde. Deren Porträts schmücken das **Vormundszimmer**, einen Salon, in dem sich einst die Apotheker in einem Dekor in reinstem flämischen Barock zur Entspannung trafen.

In het begin van de 13de eeuw, werd op het terrein van het Sint-Janshospitaal een nieuwe, grote zaal gebouwd om te voldoen aan de noden van een bevolking in volle groei. De **zolder boven de ziekenzaal** is bedekt met een imposant gebinte, meesterwerk van de Brugse ambachtslui. Men is meteen geneigd het te vergelijken met de structuur van de schepen die de havenstad aandeden.

Hans Memling was afkomstig uit Selingenstadt, bij Frankfurt-am-Main. Hij werd in de registers van de bourgeoisie in Brugge ingeschreven in 1465, wat aantoont dat hij reeds enige tijd in de stad verbleef. Zijn beroemdste werk is het **Ursulaschrijn**, in de vorm van een gotische kapel waarvan de panelen het verhaal vertellen van de reis en het martelaarschap van de Heilige en haar gezellen.

Een bourgeois decor omgeeft de **H. Maagd met het kind** maar doet niets af aan haar verhevenheid. Een open raam op het landelijke uitzicht geeft het schilderij nog meer diepte. De Maagd zit in dezelfde kamer als de schenker, de Bruggeling Maarten van Nieuwenhove, die toen drieëntwintig jaar oud was. Vijf jaar later zou hij schepen worden te Brugge en daarna, in 1497, burgemeester.

Deze triptiek werd in 1479 geschonken door Jan Floreins, die Directeur was van het Hospitaal. Het centrale paneel stelt de **Aanbidding der Wijzen** voor, geschilderd door Memling. De mystieke emotie staat te lezen op het gelaat van de koning, die de voeten van het Kind Jezus kust, terwijl Balthazar een sierlijk gebaar maakt dat Jozef enigszins aanmatigend bekijkt. De achtergrond laat een Middeleeuwse stad zien.

Au début du XIIIᵉ siècle, une nouvelle et vaste salle fut édifiée sur les terres de l'hôpital Saint-Jean pour répondre aux besoins d'une population en pleine croissance. Le **grenier au-dessus de la salle des malades** est recouvert par une imposante charpente, chef-d'œuvre des artisans brugeois. On ne peut manquer de l'imaginer pareille à la structure des vaisseaux qui fréquentaient la cité portuaire.

Originaire de Selingenstadt près de Francfort-sur-Main, Hans Memling était inscrit sur les registres de la bourgeoisie de Bruges en 1465 ce qui indique qu'il résidait depuis un certain temps dans la ville. Son œuvre la plus célèbre est la **châsse de sainte Ursule**, en forme de chapelle gothique dont les panneaux racontent le voyage et le martyre de la sainte et de ses compagnes.

Un décor bourgeois entoure la **Vierge à la pomme** mais ne le dépouille pas de sa majesté. Une fenêtre ouverte sur un paysage champêtre ajoute de la profondeur au tableau. La Vierge occupe la même pièce que le donateur, le Brugeois Maarten van Nieuwenhove alors âgé de vingt-trois ans. Cinq ans plus tard, il devint échevin de Bruges puis, en 1497, bourgmestre.

Le panneau central du triptyque offert en 1479 par Jan Floreins, qui fut Maître de l'Hôpital, constitue la plus belle **Adoration des mages** peinte par Memling. L'émotion mystique se lit sur le visage du roi qui baise les pieds de l'Enfant Jésus, tandis que Balthasar esquisse un geste de danseur que Joseph observe avec une certaine morgue. Le fond de la scène laisse entrevoir une ville médiévale.

A huge new hall was built on the grounds of Saint John's hospital at the beginning of the 13th century to meet the needs of a constantly increasing population. The **attic above the sick ward** is covered by an imposing roof, a masterpiece of Bruges artisans, recalling the hulls of the ships frequenting the city.

Hans Memling, who came from Selingenstadt near Frankfort-on Main, was entered in the register of the burghers of Bruges in 1465, indicating that he had resided for some time in the city. His most famous work is the **reliquary of Saint Ursula** in the shape of a Gothic chapel, the panels of which relate the voyage and martyrdom of the saint and her companions.

The **Virgin with an apple** sits in a comfortable middle-class decor which detracts nothing from her majesty. A window opening on a country landscape adds depth to the painting. In the same room as the Virgin is the donor, Maarten van Nieuwenhove of Bruges, then 23 years old. Five years later he became an alderman of Bruges and then in 1497, burgomaster.

The central panel of the triptych donated in 1497 by Jan Floreins, Master of the Hospital, is the most beautiful **Adoration of the Magi** painted by Memling. Mystical emotion bathes the face of the King kissing the feet of the Infant Jesus, Balthazar advances on tip-toe while Joseph looks on bemusedly. In the background is a mediaeval village.

Anfang des 13. Jhs. wurde auf dem Gelände des St. Johannes-Hospitals ein neuer großer Saal errichtet, um den Bedürfnissen einer sich in vollem Wachstum befindenden Bevölkerung nachzukommen. Der **Speicher über dem Krankensaal** ist mit einem imposanten Dachstuhl, einem Meisterwerk der Brügger Handwerker, versehen. Dessen Anblick erinnert unweigerlich an die Struktur der Schiffe, die damals in die Hafenstadt einliefen.

Hans Memling, der ursprünglich aus Selingenstadt bei Frankfurt-am-Main kam, wurde im Jahre 1465 in den Verzeichnissen der Bürgerschaft von Brügge geführt, was darauf hindeutet, dass er bereits seit einiger Zeit in dieser Stadt wohnte. Sein berühmtestes Werk ist der **Schrein der hl. Ursula** in Form einer gotischen Kapelle, deren Tafeln von der Reise und dem Martyrium der Heiligen und ihrer Begleiterinnen erzählen.

Die **Jungfrau mit dem Apfel** ist von einem bürgerlichen Dekor umgeben, was sie aber keineswegs ihrer Majestät beraubt. Ein geöffnetes Fenster auf eine ländliche Landschaft hin verleiht dem Gemälde Tiefe. Die Jungfrau befindet sich im selben Bildteil wie der Stifter, der damals dreiundzwanzigjährige Brügger Maarten van Nieuwenhove. Dieser wurde fünf Jahre später Schöffe von Brügge, im Jahre 1497 dann Bürgermeister.

Auf der Haupttafel des im Jahre 1479 von Jan Floreins, dem damaligen Leiter des Hospitals, gestifteten Triptychons stellte Memling die **Anbetung der Könige** dar. Das Gesicht des Königs, der die Füße des Jesuskindes küsst, zeigt mystische Ergriffenheit, während Balthasar die Geste eines Tänzers andeutet, die Joseph mit einem gewissen Hochmut beobachtet. Im Hintergrund ist eine mittelalterliche Stadt zu erkennen.

Begijnhof

Van de twee torens die de ingang naar het **Minnewater** flankeerden, blijft enkel nog de Poertoren (1398) overeind. Het Minnewater vormde een meer in een lager gelegen terrein en was een stroomopwaarts van Brugge gelegen handelsplaats. Belangrijke personages die naar Brugge kwamen legden daar aan, zo ook tsaar Peter de Grote in 1687.

In 1275 werd het tot dan toe geïsoleerde terrein dat "de Wijngaard" werd genoemd binnen de stadsgrenzen opgenomen. Vijftig jaar eerder hadden arme jongedames zich daar geïnstalleerd in associatie met de begijnen. Zij legden niet dezelfde geloften af als de religieuzen maar leden een altruïstisch bestaan, onder de heerschappij van de Grootjuffrouw. Sinds het begin van de 20ste eeuw woont in het begijnhof een congregatie van Benedictijnen in plaats van begijnen.
Men kan het begijnhof binnengaan via de **Wijngaardplaats** langs een ezelsbruggetje dat naar een monumentaal portaal leidt (1776). Tegenwoordig krijgt het pleintje veel toeristen op bezoek die worden aangetrokken door kantwinkeltjes ; het kantklossen is een specialiteit van de begijnen en blijft zeer nauw verbonden met het imago van Brugge.

Een veertigtal witte huizen omzomen een groot grasveld met populieren. Nadat het **begijnhof** in de 15de eeuw een welvarende periode had gekend, onderging het in de volgende eeuw de gevolgen van religieuze moeilijkheden. De 17de en de 18de eeuw luidden een nieuw periode van bloei in voor het begijnhof, maar de leden werden op een andere wijze geronseld. Bij de arme begijnen, die leefden van de inkomsten van hun werk, kwamen meer en meer begijnen uit de adel of de hogere bourgeoisie. De kleine lage huisjes maakten plaats voor mooie verblijven waar devotie geen belemmering was voor comfort, zoals het mooie gothische huis *(linkerbladzijde)* met driepasbogen dat in de 17de eeuw werd gebouwd.

Béguinage

Des deux tours flanquant l'entrée de l'étang du **Minnewater**, seule la *Poertoren* (la poudrière, 1398) se dresse encore. Formant un lac dans une dépression du terrain, le *Minnewater* constituait un bassin de commerce en amont de Bruges. Les grands personnages se rendant à Bruges y débarquaient, notamment le tsar Pierre le Grand en 1687.

Jusqu'alors isolé, le territoire appelé *de Wijngaard* (la Vigne) fut englobé dans les limites de la ville en 1275. Cinquante ans auparavant, des jeunes filles pauvres s'y étaient installées en association de béguines. Celles-ci ne prononçaient pas de vœux semblables à ceux des religieuses mais menaient, sous l'autorité de la Grande Dame, une existence altruiste. Depuis le début du XXᵉ siècle, le béguinage est occupé par une congrégation de moniales Bénédictines et non plus par des béguines.
On accède au béguinage depuis la **Wijngaardplaats** par un pont en dos d'âne qui mène au porche monumental (1776). La petite place voit aujourd'hui affluer les touristes attirés par les magasins de dentelles ; la confection de celles-ci était une spécialité des béguines et reste étroitement associée à l'image de Bruges.

Une quarantaine de maisons blanches entourent une vaste pelouse plantée de peupliers. Après avoir connu une période de prospérité au XVᵉ siècle, le **béguinage** subit, au siècle suivant, les conséquences des troubles religieux. Les XVIIᵉ et XVIIIᵉ siècles marquèrent un nouvel essor du béguinage mais son recrutement se modifia. Aux béguines peu nanties sinon pauvres, qui vivaient des revenus de leur travail, s'ajoutèrent de plus en plus de béguines nobles ou de la haute bourgeoisie. Les petites maisons basses cédèrent la place à de belles demeures où la dévotion n'excluait pas le confort, telle la belle maison de style gothique *(page de gauche)* aux remplages trilobés édifiée au XVIIᵉ siècle.

Béguinage

Only the *"Poertoren"* (powder magazine) of 1398 remains of the two towers once flanking the entrance to the **Minnewater** pond. The Minnewater, a little lake filling a depression was a commercial basin downstream from Bruges. Prominent people visiting Bruges landed there, most notably Czar Peter the Great in 1687.

The once isolated territory called the Vine fell within the extended city limits in 1275. Fifty years earlier impoverished young women had settled there, forming an association of béguines. They did not take religious vows but led an altruistic life under the rule of the Great Lady.
Since the early 20th century the béguinage has been occupied by a chapter of Benedictine nuns and not by béguines. The béguinage is approached from **Wijngaardplaats** by a humpbacked bridge leading to a monumental entrance porch (1776). The leafy little square now welcomes tourists attracted to the lace shops; lacemaking was a béguine speciality and remains closely associated with Bruges.

Forty odd houses surround a large lawn planted with poplars. After a prosperous period in the 15th century the **béguinage** suffered the consequences of the religious strife of the following century. In 1584 its church was burned down and then rebuilt in 1605 in the baroque style *(left page, background)*. In the 17th and 18th centuries the béguinage again prospered but the type of person entering changed. To the poor béguines or those of limited means were added more and more noble or upper class women. The low little houses gave way to more substantial ones where devotion did not exclude comfort, such as the pretty Gothic style house *(page left)* with trefoil insets built in the 17th century.

Beginenhof

Von den beiden Türmen, die den Zugang zum Weiher **Minnewater** flankierten, steht nur noch der *"Poertoren"* (Pulverturm, 1398). Das *Minnewasser*, das in einer Senkung des Geländes einen See bildet, diente als Handelsbecken oberhalb von Brügge. Bei ihren Besuchen in Brügge gingen dort die großen Persönlichkeiten an Land, insbesondere Zar Peter der Große im Jahre 1687.

Das bis dahin isoliert gelegene Gebiet mit Namen *Wijngaard* (Weingarten) wurde 1275 in die Begrenzungen der Stadt eingeschlossen. Fünfzig Jahre zuvor hatten sich dort arme junge Mädchen gemeinsam mit Beginen niedergelassen. Letztere legten nicht wie die Nonnen ein entsprechendes Gelübde ab, führten aber gleichwohl unter der Obrigkeit der Großen Dame ein selbstloses Dasein. Seit Anfang des 20. Jhs. wird der Beginenhof von Nonnen des Benediktinerordens und nicht länger von Beginen bewohnt.
Man betritt den Beginenhof vom **Wijngaardplaats** aus über eine gewölbte Brücke, die in die gewaltige Portalvorhalle führt (1776). Auf dem kleinen Platz strömen heute die Touristen zusammen, um die Geschäfte für Spitzenware zu besuchen; die Spitzenklöppelei war eine Spezialität der Beginen und bleibt eng mit dem Bild von Brügge verbunden.

Rund vierzig weiße Häuser umgeben eine mit Pappeln bepflanzte große Rasenfläche. Nach einer Phase des Wohlstandes im 15. Jh. bekam der **Beginenhof** im darauffolgenden Jahrhundert die Folgen der religiösen Unruhen zu spüren. Das 17. und 18. Jahrhundert brachte der Beginengemeinschaft einen neuen Aufschwung, doch deren Zusammensetzung änderte sich. Zu den wenig wohlhabenden, nicht gar armen Beginen, die von den Einkünften ihrer Arbeit lebten, gesellten sich zunehmend aus dem Adel oder dem Großbürgertum stammende Beginen hinzu. Die kleinen, niedrigen Häuser wichen schönen Wohnsitzen, bei denen die Frömmigkeit den Komfort nicht ausschloss, wie etwa dem im 17. Jh. erbauten hübschen Haus in gotischem Stil *(linke Seite)* mit Kleeblatt-Maßwerk.

© 2001 b.v.b.a. UITGEVERIJ MERCKX EDITIONS s.p.r.l.
Beeldhouwerslaan 145A, B-1180 Brussel
Avenue des Statuaires 145A, B-1180 Bruxelles

☎ 02/374.41.56
Fax 32/2/375.80.37

Photos	© Vincent Merckx
	(pages 87-89,96: Brugge, Stedelijke dienst musea)
Texts	Georges-Henri Dumont
Photo assistant	Philippe Molitor
Nederlandse bewerking	Alpha Translation
English translation	Sheila Tessier-Lavigne
Deutsche Übersetzung	DSDB
Photocomposition	Deloge (Brussels)
Photoengraving	Techniscan (Grimbergen)
Printing	Daneels (Beerse)

D-2001-0398-27
ISBN 90-74847-27-7

▷
Jan van Eyck: portret van een jonge vrouw
Jan van Eyck: portrait de jeune femme
Jan van Eyck: portrait of a young woman
Jan van Eyck: Bildnis einer jungen Frau